D R U S S I A

LITTLE

TAR...

BUDZIAC

TARTAR...

ISlam

Neister R.

Bog R.

Jaey

Lapuezna

Niz

Zerna

Bender Berlad

Belgered

OAVLA BESSARIA

ucaria Kilia Nova

ilcoz Sinila

Hajar

Korsgdin

Oblucice Tilia

Turkisin Sulu

Dorostero Silu

Kieteriha sala

atracan Wara

Tomi Mankalia

Bultham

YBantzak Kallal

Seraio

Adrianople

Attabuli

NS TAN TINOPLE

Heraclea Scutari

Galtipoli Sea of

Sesto Marmora

The Dardanelles

Troy

Smyrna

Madre R.

Lenge

Sarabat R.

B L A C K   S E A

A OF

PH

oman

Kartz Karabes Straits of Kaffa

CRIM Botusnaf

Belbeg Kaffa

Bosphorus of Thrace

K E Y   I N   A S I A

T U R K E Y   I N   A S I A

The
Liquid Continent
A Mediterranean Trilogy
Volume III: Istanbul

48

46

44

42

40

38

THE AMERICAN LIBRARY

10, RUE DU GÉNÉRAL CAMOU
75007 PARIS

The Liquid Continent

Volume III
Istanbul

The Liquid Continent

A Mediterranean Trilogy

Volume III

Istanbul

by
Nicholas Woodsworth

 Armchair Traveller

HAUS PUBLISHING
London

Copyright © 2008 Nicholas Woodsworth

First published in Great Britain in 2008 by Haus Publishing
Limited, 26 Cadogan Court, Draycott Avenue, London SW3 3BX
www.hauspublishing.co.uk

The moral rights of the author have been asserted.

A CIP catalogue record for this book is available from the British
Library

ISBN 978-1-905791-58-3

Typeset in Garamond 3 by MacGuru Ltd
Printed and bound by Graphicom in Vicenza, Italy
Jacket illustration and interior drawings courtesy of Jaroslaw
Dobrowolski (© 2008 Jaroslaw Dobrowolski)

*To Charles Woodsworth, somewhere out on a
Larrimac fairway*

One

In the Italian port of Ancona, 150 miles along the Adriatic coast from Venice, I bought a British Sunday paper. It was half a week old but hefty enough to keep me going all day. I had time to kill.

I'd spent the previous afternoon on a train plodding slowly across a wide, flat plain. Provincial, semi-industrial Italy had dragged by my window, its aging assembly plants and housing estates backing directly onto the rail tracks. Seen from its rear end, small-town life on the lower Po looked supremely dull and ugly. It was as dreary inside the train as out. Heads lolled and mouths fell open – even the locals preferred to sleep through it.

At Rimini things promised to pick up; the railway rejoined the Adriatic and ran for miles beside the open sea. But the resort towns were tacky and the water was cloudy and mud-coloured. At the Hotel Dorico in Ancona I asked for a room away from the noisy street. The hotel, though, was like the places I'd been passing through all afternoon – its back end was even less attractive than its front. After sunset a guard-dog tied to a chain-link fence began barking. The racket dragged on through the night, every link in the fence rattling as the dog hurled itself at shadows. After Venice it was all a bit of a let-down, and in the morning I discovered I had fourteen hours to hang around in Ancona. The next ferry across the Adriatic to Split did not leave until late evening.

It was a long time to wait. Even without luggage to haul around, the city, a traffic-ridden place pressed between high hills and the sea, offered few diversions. In the 15th century Pope Pius II, admittedly unwell even before he arrived from Rome on his way to yet one more Crusade, died of old age as he waited to sail from Ancona. My case wasn't as serious. But as I installed myself in a café near the water I looked at the long day stretching before me. Terminal boredom loomed.

I worked my way through the newspaper. I caught up on the latest royal indiscretion. I learned how to accessorise my garden pond with Japanese carp. I was warned off investing in vintage Bordeaux wines. By the time I came to the travel pages I was nodding. But I woke up when I turned to a colour-photo splash of an old stone house sitting over a bright blue sea.

Never mind high-rise living on the Côte d'Azur, advised a fulsome feature writer. Forget golf-course residences in Marbella and luxury time-shares on the Costa Smeralda. There was a new place where the fashionable set was investing in the Mediterranean these days. There was still time, in fact, to buy afford-able waterfront property there. But the prediction was that the supply wouldn't last – the quickening trail of investors along that hottest new Riviera, the Croatian coast, was turning into a horde.

The article bothered me. If the Croatian coast was in the Sunday papers it was far too late for me to be on the ground itself. I'd had about as much international tourism as I could stand in Venice. The idea of travelling a seashore gearing up for a summer onslaught was enough to give me hives.

What I needed was a tour of a touristless coast, a Mediterranean place no foreigner in his right mind would dream of visiting. It wasn't easy – even Colonel Qadhafi welcomed tourists with open arms these days.

There was always Gaza, I considered as I flipped my way idly through the news pages. It wasn't quite what I was looking for. Gaza might be Mediterranean, but it was a Mediterranean of violent division and dissolution. What I was searching for were traces of an older sea, a place more integrated, more inclusive than it is now.

Of course tourist-mobbed Venice, and now the Croatian coast, were part of the Mediterranean, and part of today's larger globalised world. Even the fact that I could sit on the Italian coast and read about Japanese carp and Bordeaux wines in a locally-bought British newspaper were part of that. But ever since I'd arrived in Alexandria almost six months earlier I'd been coming across the remains of a much older globalisation. It was economic, like our own, but it was more than that, too. The great Mediterranean ports of the past had been the global cities of their age. But they hadn't just connected the known world through commerce – they'd traded in an open market of ideas as well, invested in a beneficially shared outlook. They'd made the Mediterranean cosmopolitan. It was this Mediterranean, or at least what might be left of it, that I was hoping to find at the eastern end of the sea, in Istanbul. In the meantime, though, the problem was getting there without being deluged in a tidal wave of tourism.

My eyes came to a halt over a short, two-inch newspiece. A people-smuggling ring had been smashed in Germany. It was run by the same men who'd lately muscled their way into much of the organised crime in Europe. They were vicious, they were violent, and there was nothing to which they would not stoop. They were Albanian.

Now there was a thought. I'd never heard of Albanian tourism, never seen advertising luring visitors to the romantic and sunny Illyrian coast. Come to think of it, I'd never heard of a single Albanian attraction apart from Mother Teresa. Perhaps here was the solution to the summer crowds of the Mediterranean. But I hesitated. This was a British Sunday paper, after all. Off I trotted to verify the story of Albanian bad guys at an internet café up the road.

Unsurprisingly, I found nothing about Albanian tourism. But the nasty character of the Albanian Mafia was unstintingly confirmed in dozens of web-pages. There was an Italian prosecutor who'd identified Albanian thugs as a major threat to Western society – 'The road for drugs and arms and people, meaning illegal immigrants to Europe, is in Albanian hands,' he'd said. In Poland Albanians had cornered the market in Ecstasy distribution. In former Yugoslavia they smuggled petrol. On the Georgian border, conducting business with the Russian army, they traded heroin for heavy weapons. Even in Soho, in the heart of civilised London, the Albanians were busy – the Metropolitan Police estimated that nearly three quarters of all women working in UK brothels were Albanians or Albanian Kosovars.

If the Albanian Mafia had been able to pull that off on the far side of the continent, I wondered, what kind of havoc they had they managed to wreak in their own backyard? Of course nobody went holidaying in Albania. It was the perfect Mediterranean stop *en route* to Istanbul.

I was at the ferry ticket office down in the port ten minutes later. There were at least half a dozen companies running in and out of Ancona – Jadrolinija to Split and Zara; Minoan Lines to Greece; the Blue Line; Anek; SNAV. The queue for the overnight ferry to Split wouldn't start forming for hours, but there was a line tailing back from the Superfast Ferries counter, and it was so restive that there was obviously a ferry about to leave.

'Where are you going?' I asked a short, grizzled man in a black suit standing at the back of the queue.

'Igoumenitsa!' he smiled broadly. He looked so happy about it that Igoumenitsa or parts thereabout had to be home.

'What time does the ferry leave?' I said, stepping into line behind him. I wasn't exactly sure where

Igoumenitsa was, but the man was flipping a set of worry-beads. He looked Greek. That was good enough for me – anything was better than another ten hours in an Ancona café.

'Now! Now!' he replied, looking at his watch. My question only made him more anxious that he would miss the sailing. In fact there were still a few minutes left. From my bag I fished out my map of the eastern Mediterranean and searched for Igoumenitsa. It lay behind Corfu on the Greek mainland, just south of the Albanian border. A quarter of an hour later I was in front of the counter, asking about accommodation for the eighteen-hour trip. After a night in the Hotel Dorico I thought I deserved a small treat, and told the the ticket lady so.

'For €271 you can have an outside cabin with double bed, television, fridge, hair dryer and in-cabin breakfast,' she replied. 'It's a good price. In high season it's €380. It's a luxury cabin.'

€271 would have bought me more than a month's stay in the Union Hotel in Alexandria. It was a little more luxury than I needed, I told her.

She shrugged. 'Then you can have a reclining seat for €61.' I shook my head. That didn't sound much better than the Dorico.

She lowered her voice. 'I wouldn't take either of them,' she confided. 'The boat is almost empty. Take a bed in a six-berth compartment. There will be no one else there.'

€98 and five minutes later I was climbing aboard the *Superfast XI*.

The ferry was red and white, newly built and squeaky-clean. There wasn't a scuff mark on it. There was chrome and mirrored glass everywhere. Acres of thick carpeting stretched away into the distance. The vessel was 656 feet long, towered ten decks high, and could carry 1,500 passengers and 900 vehicles. And it was, as promised, superfast – it shot up and down the Adriatic at 31 knots, more than 35 miles an hour.

But what the ferry was not, at this time of year, was busy. The lounges were empty, the cafeterias abandoned, the bars deserted. I dropped down a couple of decks to dump my bag. When I swiped my key-card in a door and entered a communal accommodation area not a soul had claimed any of the half-dozen compartments inside. I felt reprieved, like a long-haul air passenger who suddenly stumbles onto a whole row of empty seats to stretch out on.

I stood at the rails of the stern sundeck, watching the last vehicles roll into the *Superfast XI*'s hold. Tourists might be seasonal, but provisioning Europe's factories, firms and supermarkets was a year-round affair. There were ten times more commercial trucks and drivers boarding the ferry than private cars and passengers. Eurostar Transport, Continental Food and Flowers, Logistics Mars, Olympic Flame International, Floridis Meat Industries, Brinkman Trucking of Holland ... Ancona may have lacked interest for idlers like me, but for businesses across the continent it was a busy international transport-hub.

You only had to look at the couple of hundred trucks pulled up in the port parking lot, wavy lines of heat pouring from exhaust stacks above their cabs, to realise how connected the different parts of Europe had become. Politics was something else – the French could moan about the English, New Europe could stand up to Old Europe and the whole lot of them could bitch about Brussels. But in the meantime they were all happy to go on eating each other's food, wearing each other's shoes and buying each other's cars. You didn't have to ask the crew of brawny truck-drivers ascending from parking bays silly questions about what was going to make Europe work or not work. They already knew.

My only complaint was that the whole thing was so completely aseptic. I wandered for a few minutes. There was a video-game area with banks of flashing screens and synthesized sound effects – they introduced passengers to light entertainments with names like 'Armageddon' and 'Death Wish III'. There was a casino with more serried ranks of machines – one-armed bandits and electronic roulette tables – also awaiting fresh infusions of Euro coins. There was an Internet Corner, a brightly-coloured children's playroom, a whole slew of sparkling-clean buffets, self-service cafeterias and *à la carte* restaurants. There were more television viewing areas than I could count.

There were lounge-bars, a discotheque, a swimming pool, boutiques selling jewellery and name-brand fragrances. The *Superfast XI*, halfway between a utilitarian transport ferry and a sumptuous cruise liner, was anodyne and anonymous. It had all the character features of an international airport. Even its name spoke of something stamped out in series – presumably there were at least ten other similar vessels ploughing ferry routes on other seas.

I re-emerged onto the stern sundeck to see ropes being cast off and cables running through hawsers onto drums. Slowly the *Superfast XI* moved away from the quay and began churning water. We crawled past port installations running out on a long mole. There were tall yellow cranes, grain and cement silos, gondola-cars moving down a rail spur. A boat basin full of commercial fishing vessels came into view beside the ferry port, then a freight terminal piled high with shoebox-shaped freight containers. We passed the *Halo Cygnus*, a bulky black container carrier registered in Panama, being loaded by the quay. Behind her the *Romania II*, out of Monrovia, was lying low in the water and waiting to be unloaded. Finally we were away. The ferry picked up speed and the green hills behind Ancona began to grow smaller. Fifteen minutes from the port we crossed a line, so distinct that it might have been laid out with a pencil and ruler, dividing on-shore waters from the open sea. The first I'd already seen from the train – a mucky brown effluvium washed into the sea over recent days of heavy rain. But the water that lay beyond it was the purest Mediterranean blue, a clear, deep aquamarine whose surface now foamed to a creamy white froth behind us.

I sat out on the deck in warm sunshine and day-dreamed most of the afternoon away. Occasionally there were glimpses of the low-lying Italian coast. Mostly, though, there was nothing, just bright sky and bright sea and an empty horizon. Few other passengers came outdoors. Of the truck drivers there wasn't a sign – they had their own designated lounges and as a superior class remained apart from the dross of ordinary humanity. I was happy enough just to watch our wide wake recede, a dazzling, spumey ribbon fading first to a velvety blue, then to nothing. We were eating up the miles.

Around sunset it grew cool and I moved indoors. I drank a beer at the bar and had dinner in a brightly lit, virtually deserted restaurant. After dinner I watched a middle-aged couple, the sole occupants of the dance-floor, revolve in the spangly light of a mirrored disco-ball twirling from the ceiling.

I turned in early, thinking about our 5.30 a.m. arrival in Igoumenitsa. And also because there wasn't a single television screen, video game, fruit machine or boutique service I wished to avail myself of. The sheets in my berth were snowy white and crisply ironed, the calm absolute. But I regretted that human cargoes were moved about these days with as much emotion as steel-bound container cargoes. For a moment I was tempted to think almost fondly of that other ferry I'd taken, the rusty Saudi hulk that made the run from Egyptian Nuweiba up the Gulf of Aqaba.

What the *Superfast XI* needed, I decided as I dropped off to sleep, was a surprise boarding by a thousand or so clamorous Arabs, wild-eyed and wind-whipped in their travel-stained *galabiyas*. They might not please the occupants of the luxury outside cabins as they lay on double beds blow-drying their hair. But they would certainly add a little zing to modern Mediterranean ferry travel.

Two

A highly developed sense of self and personal honour; a fierce allegiance to family and clan; a strong attachment to tradition and the past – no one admires these qualities more than I. They are the foundation of Mediterranean society, the firm sea floor to which Mediterraneans anchor themselves as the currents of history slop and swirl about them. They give the people of this sea a certain stability and order.

Unfortunately, they also give it a certain disorder. For as often as not Mediterraneans couldn't care less about anything that falls outside these narrow allegiances. I needn't have lamented too much the passing of an older way of life aboard the *Superfast XI*. I was on my way to Albania, and the screw-you-Jack, what'sit-to-me unruliness of the Levant was even closer than I thought.

On the early morning bus from Igoumenitsa to Ioannina, the inland town where I would catch another bus to the Albanian border, we crossed a range of high coastal hills. Scattered with wildflowers in late spring, still fresh and green before the searing heat of summer, they were glorious. I am not sure the bus driver saw them that way. I am not sure he saw them at all. From his side-window he flung out into the morning, at intervals, his styrofoam coffee cup, a chocolate-bar wrapper, a handful of paper tissues and an empty plastic water bottle. Perhaps he didn't see the no-smoking sign above his head either, for next he lit up a cigarette and threw out the just-finished packet for good measure. Nobody paid any attention – the ditches outside were full of this kind of stuff. Things only got messier from there.

The men who boarded the next bus in Ioannina weren't just slovenly in their attentions to the countryside. They weren't too fastidious about themselves, either. Unshaven and sweaty, they wore grubby suits bagged out at knee and elbow, broken shoes and white shirts with grime-ringed collars. Some of them looked as if they had been travelling for days. At the border they pulled out Albanian passports and were treated disdainfully by Greek customs officials. They didn't look like violent and vicious Mafia thugs to me. They looked like tired, overworked migrant labourers anxious to get home.

We walked a quarter of a mile through a tree-stripped no-man's-land. 'Tourism,' an Albanian customs official intoned slowly, once I was on the far side of the barricades, observation towers and coiled razor-wire that made up the frontier. As if in some doubt he knitted his brows as he read and stamped the immigration card I'd filled in. It didn't look like he processed tourist entries very often. Overall, I got the feeling more people were trying to get out of Albania than get in.

The next man I spoke to was much more positive. 'Welcome in Albania!' crowed Ermir Bejkollari, a smile on his plump, moustachioed face as he opened the front door of his minivan. He meant it, too – he immediately hustled the old woman sitting beside the driver's seat into the back with the other passengers. It was no good protesting. I was his personal charge until we got to Tirana, and he wouldn't hear another word.

Albania, for a short while at least, seemed like a rural paradise. As we drove away from the border post there was no indication that the industrial age had ever penetrated these rugged hills. Beside meadows dark with blood-red poppies women turned drying hay with pitchforks. Men scythed grass or tilled patchwork fields with horses and iron ploughs. Dropping lines into torrents splashing with snowmelt from the mountains above, bare-footed boys fished from ancient wooden bridges. There were shepherds' huts of daubed wattle; curling rams' horns nailed to gateposts; scarecrow effigies hanging like talismans from the rafters of houses. Albania didn't appear merely pre-mechanical. It looked pre-Christian, pre-Muslim, pre- any institution that extended its requirements past basic survival and the husbandry of animals. Albania was barely formed, a pagan land buried back at the very beginning of things.

The illusion was captivating, but crumbled almost immediately. Further down the valley I could see giant puffball mushrooms two or three feet across growing in swathes. Closer up, they turned out to be low, half-domes of concrete, above-ground protection for gun-slitted foxholes buried in the earth. They were military bunkers, each built to hold a single man, and there were hundreds of them. They continued in successive defensive bands for miles down the valley. Peasant life – pastures, fruit orchards, herds of sheep – just had to work around them.

When I looked at Ermir Bejkollari for explanation he only rolled his eyes and tapped the side of his head with a forefinger. 'Big crazy!' was all he could say in English.

It wasn't long before I was beginning to think the whole country was big crazy. The first villages, no pastoral idylls, were built on the Stalinist social model – block after geometrically laid out block of flaking and decrepit cement-slab constructions. Towns were the same but larger. Garbage lay liberally strewn about. Roads were muddy and pot-holed.

Traffic was held up by horses pulling overloaded carts of fodder.

Country people got on and off. Some were pretty ripe. Near the town of Gjirokaster one old gent climbed into the van exuding an odour of unwashed body so pungent, so fermented, cured and aged that we all rolled down the windows. But sometimes it was less fragrant outside than in. We drove into a long valley that had once been an oilfield. Rusty rigs and abandoned derricks littered its slopes and floor. They'd been clumsily capped – the air was heavy and acrid, and from the base of the derricks thick black oil oozed out into pools. It ran downhill beside orchards and fields of crops, dribbled into stinking ditches and finally emptied into a river whose surface was black and iridescent with petroleum rainbows.

We drove down out of the hills and onto a more populated coastal plain, now close enough to Tirana that the capital's FM radio stations filled the van with the slick voices of American-style DJs. The music was gangsta-rap sung in Albanian.

Outside the window the bizarre mix of primitive

agriculture, abandoned industry and deserted military installations only grew more nightmarish. But as we drew near the port of Durrës Albania took on a contemporary note. The roads were now thick with jockeying traffic – in six hours we had gone from a wheel-less society to one that appeared bent on mass automotive annihilation. Odder still, most of the cars were the same make. In between Bejkollari's own attempts at suicidal passing I did a rough count – six out of ten vehicles were Mercedes. The landscape, too, assumed modern touches. There were still women out there ploughing with horses, but scattered among the fields, bunkers and smashed-up factories were new constructions.

Possibly they were resort hotels and holiday homes. They were so shoddy and gimcrack, so hastily thrown up amidst the detritus of a collapsed society that it was difficult to imagine anyone wanting to spend any free time in them. But as we arrived at the coast and ran north along the sandy sweep of the Bay of Durrës there could be no doubt – the cheap buildings erected side by side were beach hotels.

Some were open for business even as earth and rubble from construction sites next door was being piled high around them.

Albania's hysteric building boom reached a paroxysm as we swung inland for the half-hour drive to Tirana. The approaches to the city were one vast construction site. It was anarchic. Buildings sprouted everywhere. Zoning had never been heard of. There was slum housing in narrow lanes running beneath half-completed flyovers. There were shiny new car showrooms lying amidst cabbage fields. Cement-mixers, iron scaffolding and pallets of tiles lay strewn along the roadside. The roads grew more congested, drivers edgier. Car horns blared continuously. It was all getting out of hand – if these were just the suburbs, I wondered, what in God's name could I expect in the city itself?

But downtown Tirana, inexplicably, was a haven of order. There was a main square where a vast wall-mosaic had once honoured the toiling revolutionary masses; now the red star of communism that had crowned it was gone and workers and peasants were conspicuously absent in the streets below. In their place prosperous-looking urban consumers went placidly about their business. There were grassy parks, promenades, broad avenues of government ministries decorated in yellow sienna and maroon trim. The whole city centre had been spruced up – in keeping with the mood even old-style communal housing had been repainted and now looked like a bright, multi-coloured experiment in Op-Art.

Ermir Bejkollari dropped off the last of his passengers and we drove around in circles looking for a hotel. Everything was in the luxury category. I was perplexed. Here was a country where things like soap seemed out of most people's reach, yet you couldn't find a room for less than $150 a night. Finally I paid Bejkollari off – he made me promise to telephone him if nothing came up – and began to walk. Five minutes later I was registering at the Dajti Hotel. Obscured by tall pine trees, it was so gloomily monolithic I had taken it for one of the last, unreformed institutions of the old dictatorship.

It was. Just down the street the former Enver

Hoxha Museum, not long ago dedicated to the eternal memory of the Albanian dictator, had reinvented itself as the International Culture Centre. But the Hotel Dajti had been so steeped in the totalitarian spirit for so long it appeared unreformable. It had been built by other despots, Italian Fascists who'd occupied the country during the Second World War. But soon home-grown autocrats had taken it over and felt perfectly at home in its Mussolini-inspired décor. Now one of the country's last state-owned establishments, it had been communist Albania's premier hotel for half a century. Pompous and ponderous in style, everything in it spoke of decades of crushing state bureaucracy.

The reception desk dwarfed the woman who stood behind it. A grand hallway almost a hundred yards long and covered in worn red carpeting ran off into dim obscurity on either side. Lined by massive square columns, it was supposed to be illuminated by chandeliers hanging from high ceilings, but most of the light bulbs were missing. There was a conspicuous shortage of guests, too – the only people in the lobby when I arrived were two shapeless women swabbing the endless marble lobby floor with mops and buckets.

Some of the rigour of the old days must have gone, for the receptionist was quietly quaffing an afternoon glass of wine. She wasn't above a little cash bargaining, either, and I ended up with a double room for the price of a single. The Dajti was a fraction of the cost of the new hotels, but I got what I paid for. The plumbing was quirky and the furniture threadbare; maintenance was so minimal the potted palms in the lounge appeared to be suffering the effects of long-term drought. But I liked the Hotel Dajti anyway. It was about the only place in Albania I could actually understand.

How did it all fit together? I walked through the city that evening, trying to figure it out. A stone-age countryside; industry in ruins; an out-of-control building boom; a military gone mad, then just plain gone. And now this – a mystifying prosperity that let hip young Albanians splash out on a lavish scale.

I strolled around 'the Bloc', once a barricaded residential area reserved for members of the communist

27

elite. Green and leafy, it was still a place for the privileged. But now capitalists lounged around in ersatz French tea salons. They browsed pricy clothing boutiques and socialised in cafés with silly, hybrid names like the Cowboy Pub. The citizens that packed the sidewalk cafés were well-dressed and well-bathed and fragrant – there was no soap shortage here. They liked to show off other little luxuries – if there were half a dozen people sitting together in a café there were half a dozen mobile telephones piled on the table in front of them. Downtown Tirana was as trendy as any Western capital – it was just that nothing jibed with the appalling mess that lay all around it.

I considered dropping by the Boom-Boom Room, a place where live bands would keep crowds of Albanians rollicking until dawn. But it didn't get going until late, and after the long day's drive I was tired. Nobody else was. When I strolled home around midnight even the little park opposite the Hotel Dajti was still going strong. There, surrounded by illuminated splashing fountains, lay the latest in high-tech bowling alleys.

I thought bowling alleys were hang-outs for blue-collar buddies in the American rustbelt. But there was no one swigging Busch Lite from the bottle here. Inside, bowlers sat sipping exotic cocktails around tables whose glass surfaces showed their bowling scores racked up on electronic displays. A battery of wall-mounted plasma screens was tuned to Fashion TV. Justin Timberlake wailed 'Rock Your Body' through a dozen thudding multi-directional speakers. Out in the lanes, ultraviolet lights picked out eerily-lit teenagers whose orange and blue fluorescent bowling balls rolled towards pins glowing in the distance. Tirana was getting stranger and stranger. I needed some answers, fast.

I got them the next morning without ever leaving the hotel. At the rear of the Dajti lay the offices of Albturist, the Albanian state tourist organisation. The Hotel Dajti was not only Albturist's global headquarters; it was its sole public office. That didn't mean the world was beating a furious path to the Dajti's back door. When I asked to see Albtourist's general manager, Arjan Skenderi, I was shown in right away.

Mr Skenderi was a deliberate, methodical man with salt-and-pepper hair and a mustard-coloured jacket. He seemed delighted that an outsider might be interested in a concept as ephemeral as Albanian tourism.

'Of course it's difficult to understand Albania today. But it is even harder to understand Albania as it was before,' he said. He sat with his lips pursed and the fingertips of his hands lightly pressed to each other. He had the contemplative air of a man considering one of the great conundrums of his age.

'Hotels are meant to receive guests. But do you think the Dajti was run to encourage foreigners to visit Albania?' It was like a riddle from the sphinx. I didn't know how to answer. 'No!' Mr Skenderi answered for me. 'Everything was done to turn them away!'

Turning away foreigners seemed to be an Albanian speciality. Perhaps this was the moment to ask about those military bunkers.

Arjan Skenderi winced, rolling his eyes precisely the way Ermir Bejkollari had done. He seemed genuinely embarrassed. 'All dictators have their obsessions,' he said. 'Enver Hoxha's was fear of attack.

Do not ask me who was going to invade us. Nobody ever knew. But when Hoxha studied in Paris as a young man he learned about the Maginot Line. Those bunkers were our Maginot Lines. There are still more than 600,000 of them scattered along our borders. We've got to do something with them. There has even been talk of a national competition with a prize for the best suggestion. Beach-front changing rooms, Enver Hoxha souvenir telephone booths ... everyone has a different idea.'

But there were still tougher Albanian puzzles to solve, the general manager told me. When the regime collapsed in the early 1990s mayhem had set in. A decade and a half later the country had yet to emerge from it.

'After fifty years of absolute state control suddenly we were free. We felt, naturally, we had the right to do anything we liked. So that's just what we did,' Mr Skenderi said. 'No one had ever owned anything before. But just owning things wasn't enough – in the middle of collapse everyone wanted to be an entrepreneur, a rich capitalist. It was impossible to control.

There was,' he said, carefully searching for his words, 'an abusive interpretation of the market economy.'

It was masterful understatement. Out in the country, peasants appropriated the land they'd worked collectively and refused any kind of zoning or planning. More than 15 years later rural property disputes were still choking the courts. In the city things went even further out of kilter. Before 1990 only 200,000 of Albania's three million residents lived in Tirana. Over the next decade more than three times that number swamped the capital. Those who were able to get out of the country altogether did so. Soon almost a million overseas Albanians were repatriating funds and sinking them into an urban free-for-all.

'It was chaos – too much, too fast,' said Mr Skenderi. 'First it was bars, cafés and clubs. Then bigger things – the investors took over the whole city. You couldn't imagine what the downtown looked like. It's all been pulled down now, and the illegal operators driven out of the centre. Our next targets are on the city periphery. Control there has not yet been wholly re-established.'

More understatement. I mentioned the Mercedes-Benzes that clogged city streets and defied death out in the country. The manager winced again.

'Ah yes. The Mercedes ... It's a very, well ... a very *Albanian* thing. Everyone wants to look important. Under Enver Hoxha we all pedalled around on bicycles – there were only three or four hundred cars in the whole city. They belonged to officials, and they were mostly Mercedes-Benzes. So now there's an endless appetite for second-hand Mercedes. It is the vehicle of choice – for a few thousand euros you can look like an influential man.'

Maybe that's why people drove so atrociously – a decade isn't long for an entire nation to learn to shift S-500 Mercedes Sedans around hairpin Balkan bends. But I refrained from asking the man from Albturist the obvious question – where had all the money for this conspicuous consumption come from?

The pinching of attractive motor vehicles from shopping-centre parking lots across Europe could only be just the beginning of Albania's abusive market-economy interpretations. What about the gangsterism run on a continental scale, the money laundering, drug dealing, gun running, prostitution, people smuggling and sundry other forms of racket-eering? Poor Mr Skenderi, however, already seemed more than sufficiently pained – he'd already had to explain away a psychotic dictator, to say nothing of unsolvable land squabbles, urban anarchy and an unconscionable number of luxury motor cars. So I asked him instead about Albania's great hope for the future, Mediterranean tourism.

Immediately he brightened. Plans were already well advanced, he said. Of course, Greece to the south and Croatia to the north were far ahead. But the potential was there, and it was focussed on Durrës. Those chaotic beach developments I had driven past were intended for domestic tourism, for Albanian and Kosovar package holidays. But there were many more miles of beautiful coast, still untouched, reserved for an elite foreign market. Even as we spoke plans were being drawn up for half a dozen tourist villages with a thousand beds each.

I hoped the entrepreneur with the concrete-bunker

changing-room idea was not part of the tourism planning committee. What, I asked, was biggest problem for the leisure industry – money?

Arjan Skenderi shook his head. Of course funding was needed, he acknowledged – foreign investors were more than welcome to come forward. But that was not the main challenge.

'What we have to do is get away from the lure of quick profit,' the man in the mustard jacket sighed. 'There is one thing Albania really needs – a new mentality.'

The next day I took a bus back out through the confusion of suburban Tirana to the old port of Durrës. Once it was the starting point of the Via Egnatia, the Roman road linking Rome to Constantinople. Much later, too, it was a major Venetian trading port. For a few years in the early 20th century it was even the capital of Albania. But all that, like the Durrës of the future, had to be imagined.

Behind the Durrës bus station a narrow lane ran towards the harbour. It ended in a kind of make-shift waiting area, an open, muddy place pressed up against a railway track and the high fence that surrounded the port. Flimsy chairs and refreshment stands thrown together from wood and plastic sheeting shared the area with piles of refuse. A guard stood at a metal gate in the fence, blocking the only way forward.

Where, I asked a man slithering through the mud on a bicycle, was the main passenger entrance to the Durrës ferry terminal?

Right here, he said.

Could this possibly be the first taste of Albania for sea-travellers arriving from across the Adriatic, I wondered? It seemed so doubtful I went back to the lane and enquired at a ticket kiosk there. The man behind the counter threw up his hands.

'What do you want?' he said. 'This port belongs to thieves and corrupt officials.' He didn't seem to share Arjan Skenderi's optimism for the future. 'When Hoxha fell 20,000 people sailed from Albania in any boat they could find.' He pointed out to sea and the Straights of Otantro. 'Brindisi lies just there, 120 kilometres away. Do you think 20,000 people are going to come sailing back from Brindisi tomorrow? Yes, this is where ferry travellers arrive.'

If Albania was going to open its doors to tourism Durrës would have to get a move on. I walked a mile or so along the street fronting the port. Mottled and stained apartment blocks, their balconies bricked in to make extra rooms, ran along the harbour fence. Abandoned buildings, wrecked train carriages, piles of scrap metal and more concrete bunkers buried in the ground completed the air of seafront desolation. Further on, past guarded gates where transport lorries were entering the port, I saw new buildings going up. Waylaid by a drunk, I never got there. He was rheumy-eyed and crying and, latching on to my shirtsleeve, refused to let go. He'd been deported from Italy. 'Come and drink, just one drink,' he kept whining in Italian. I eventually pried his hands away and started back for the station. I'd had enough of Durrës. If there was an unhappier port in the Mediterranean I hadn't seen it.

That evening I sat on a sidewalk terrace in the Bloc drinking coffee and thinking about progress.

All around me people were relaxing after a day's hectic efforts. Trying to get ahead in any way they could, Albanians were making progress. At least a sort of progress. A saner kind of Albania was slowly spreading out from the centre of Tirana, and one day its ripples would wash up against sad and dilapidated Durrës. In the end I liked Tirana, if for nothing else than a drive and energy so rugged you could almost touch it. Albanians, there was no doubt about it, were go-getters.

And that was a good thing, if they were going to sort out the looniness that results when human contact is stifled and people become cut off from each other. For half a century Albania had been the very opposite of cosmopolitan, a state in perfect isolation. That Albanians had in the last little while become not just more cosmopolitan but unscrupulous go-getters as well – pirates, to put it plainly – was not an insurmountable problem.

For there were other Mediterraneans just up the coast who had once indulged in wholesale piracy, too. If I remembered it correctly, a major naval expedition under the Venetian Doge Pietro Orseolo had been required to curb their enthusiasm for thievery, murder, rapine and all other manner of nastiness. So relieved were the Venetian population when it came to an end that they celebrated ever after with an annual thanksgiving. And where were those once-feared Croatians today? In the travel pages of the British Sunday papers, of course.

Three

In the northern Greek port of Kavala I asked about sailings to Lesbos. The young man behind the counter, organised and efficient, barely glanced at his computer.

'There's a sailing to Mitilene tomorrow morning at five o'clock on the M.V. *Rodanthi*. It costs €23.60, and it stops at Limnos at eleven. You arrive at Mitilene at four in the afternoon.'

'But I don't want to go to Mitilene,' I said, thinking I'd been misheard. 'I want to go to Lesbos.' I pulled out my map and showed him the island, triangular and indented by a deep bay, lying just a short hop across the water from the Turkish coast. It was clearly marked 'Lesbos'.

He studied the map, then tapped it with his

finger. 'Yes, that's what I told you. You arrive at four o'clock.'

'But why do you call it Mitilene?' Lesbos was how the place was marked on all the maps and guidebooks I'd looked at.

The ticket man was now looking both self-conscious and defiant at the same time. 'Lesbos was an early name. Tourists and foreigners still use it, but Greeks prefer to use the later name.'

'Why is that?'

'Because,' he said, hesitating over an answer. 'Because we are traditional.'

I was confused. 'But if you were traditional surely you'd use the earlier name, wouldn't you?'

He'd had enough. 'No, we are traditional because we don't want to be connected with the idea of sex between women. Some people like to make a big story about Sappho on Lesbos and the kind of woman she was. But we do not. The women who live there are ordinary Greeks, wives and mothers and family women. Why should they be called Lesbians?'

'Fine,' I said. 'You're right. Forget Lesbos. I'll

take a ticket to Mitiline instead. And I'll also take a later ferry if you've got one – I find early sailings as offensive as early names. In my book five o'clock is a scandalous and indecent hour.'

The ticket man wasn't amused. But I thought his insistence on a sexually-neutral name for an island prudish. It was only a name. No one should subject old islands to modern gender issues. At any rate there were no other ferries to Lesbos/Mitiline so I settled down to spend a quiet time in Kavala waiting for the *Rodanthi*.

I didn't mind at all. I was travel-weary. I found a room overlooking the sea and with bright light bouncing up through closed shutters snoozed for half the day. The road from Tirana over the mountains into Greek Macedonia had been long. And Thessalonica, Greece's industrial second city, had been uncomfortably big and sprawling for a passer-through like me.

But Kavala was different. Too far north in the Aegean to be on the busy tourist circuit, it was one of those rare things – a Mediterranean fishing port that had kept its soul. Prosperous, relaxed and friendly, it was easy to feel at home in the little city. And it had a past, too. On the top of the hill overlooking the harbour sat a citadel with high stone towers and battlements. Over the centuries Kavala had served as the fortified base for the usual cast of Levantine defenders and attackers – Byzantines, Normans, Franks, Venetians and, of course, the longest-installed of all occupants, the Ottomans.

When I woke in the late afternoon I strolled the steep, narrow streets of the old town. There were still signs of those earlier residents. Here and there were old Ottoman private homes, the wooden lathes of their crumbling walls showing through like ribs. They were reminders, melancholy accusations against a departed but still deeply-resented occupier. Most evocative of all was a mosque in ruins, its minaret taken down and its doors closed tight with rusty locks and chains. Above, bright red wildflowers grew on a rotted roof beneath a copper finial of a crescent moon, long ago bent out of shape and never straightened.

Such neglect was hardly astonishing. In the last

century the relationship between Greek and Turk has been so bitter and vindictive that it's a surprise to see even faint traces of one people lingering on in the territory of the other.

But in Kavala there were Turkish remains that had not only survived, but prospered. On a small square I stumbled across a bronze statue of Mohammed Ali, the Muslim Kavala Albanian who had gone on to become the founder of modern Egypt. Bearded and turbaned, unsheathing a curved scimitar, he sat his fiery steed in front of the house he'd been born in. He was not the only one wielding the tool of his profession; behind him stonemasons were busy hammering and carpenters sawing – his stone house was undergoing major renovation.

There was another hive of activity further down the hill in a building known as the Imaret. Long and narrow, dimpled with stone domes and covered with carved calligraphy, it had once been an Islamic almshouse lodging students of Koranic theology. Judging from the expensive Italian kitchen ranges and cold-storage units being hefted through its doors by panting workmen, it was well on its way to a culinary future.

Down at the port, I shared the setting sun with a leisurely crowd of Kavala citizens on their evening promenade. The only really busy individuals on the waterfront just then were hundreds of diving, looping swallows and the crews of two fishing boats preparing to head out to sea. The *Stephanos Manios* and *Constantinus B* were eighty-foot *lamparo* boats, the skiffs on their decks fitted with acetylene tanks and bright lamps for night-fishing. Dressed in tracksuits and cheap plastic sandals, their crews were loading ice and preparing for a long, cold night out on the open water. Not one was Greek. They were all Egyptians, Muslims from the coastal cities of Port Said and Damietta.

I stood watching their last-minute work with a knot of well-covered, elderly Greeks, men who fifty years ago would themselves have been setting out to spend the night fishing. One had a sister in Newcastle. 'Newcastle! Po! Po! Po!' he said to me. 'Too wet, too cold for Greeks!' I asked him about the renovations to the old Ottoman buildings on the hill above the port.

He laughed out loud. 'It is easy,' he said and, holding out his hand, rubbed his thumb and forefinger together.

'It's money. They are worth a fortune. No Greek can do such beautiful work in stone these days. You have seen the changes at the Imaret. And Mohammed Ali's house is being turned into a hotel by a wealthy woman – it will soon have a bar and a swimming pool and luxury suites. As for the Egyptian fishing crews, they go out in all weathers for long hours, summer and winter, and they are paid very little. Local men don't want to do that anymore. We Greeks say history is sacred. I say there are times when money is more sacred to us than history.'

The next morning the *Rodanthi* not only left at an indecent hour; she was, quite literally, a smutty old ship. Heavy black cinders flew from her rusty smokestack as soon as we cleared the harbour. At first I didn't see them in the half-light, but before Kavala was out of sight my shirt was covered with thick smudges. Soon the rear deck where passengers walked was a mess of long black streaks and I moved upwind to the bows to escape the hail of ash. I am glad I did. I had never seen Mediterranean porpoises before. Now they were dancing and diving before the ship's bow-wave, as old as mythical Greece itself and as fresh and bright as the morning that enveloped us. They made getting up early worth it.

The day was long, the *Rodanthi* late, and before I set out for Molyvos at the far north end of Lesbos the island's buses had stopped running. But hitch-hiking the forty miles of winding hill roads to Molyvos wasn't difficult. I had rides with a soldier, a salesman and – I dare not say three Lesbians – three island-women returning home from a shopping expedition. It was almost dark when I arrived.

Molyvos was worth the effort, too. In no time I was sitting on a balcony high over the town, looking out at red-tiled roofs and a darkening sea to the shores of Anatolia. In the little walled and marble-flagged courtyard below me, Maria Karanikoli's husband was trimming garden-grown vegetables for the evening meal. The landlady herself was tending to her flowers – roses and geraniums, pansies and hydrangeas and fuchsias – all growing in big terracotta pots. The rooms she rented above her family's ground-floor quarters were comfortable and spotless, and apart from mine, empty. On the quay at Molyvos' miniature harbour that evening, with tourists bobbing by on one side and boats on the other, I drank retsina, ate calamari, and went to bed happy. There is nothing quite as Greek as a Greek port.

But in fact Molyvos's past was even less Greek than Kavala's. Molyvos was, quite simply, a Turkish town. Having wrested Lesbos from Genoese control less than a decade after the fall of Constantinople, Sultan Mehmet II used the island as a place to reward deserving Janissary troops with retirement and property.

In the late 1400s one of these resettled Janissaries married the widow of a Greek priest on Lesbos and there produced six children. Two of these offspring went on to change Mediterranean history. One of them founded the kingdom of Algeria far to the west. The other, known as Barbarossa, became Captain General of the Ottoman fleet under Suleiman the Magnificent. Drawing on years of experience in piracy – not only Croats were good at that game – Barbarossa transformed the Turkish navy. And with it he turned the central and eastern Mediterranean into a Turkish sea.

Molyviots could hardly hide the Turkish origins of their town. Touristy but well-preserved, shaded by trellised foliage, its streets were overhung by upper stories protruding outwards in typical Ottoman style. There were Turkish fountains, Turkish inscriptions carved in stone, Turkish baths that once formed the social centre of the town. But no local would ever tell you that the most feared admiral in Turkish naval history was the son of a Lesbos woman once married to a Greek Orthodox priest. Molyviots would rather die first.

From Molyvos Turkey may fill the entire eastern horizon, but islanders avoid mentioning it at all. Officially the country didn't seem to exist. In municipal tourist-office brochures the island sat not off Turkey but off the coast of Asia Minor. The failed 1922 Greek invasion of Turkey was the 'Asia Minor Disaster'. Local food, drawing heavily like all Greek food on Turkish cooking, had 'near-eastern' influences. And in a travel agency down by the port one didn't visit Turkey – one took, as a poster in the window coyly put it, 'a day-trip to the Orient'.

If the T-word was scrupulously avoided it was more difficult, despite the reticence of the ticket agent in Kavala, to avoid the L-word. In recent years the island has become a summer pilgrimage for European lesbians. Locals themselves may not subscribe to the sexual preferences of their 6th-century BC poetess, but Sappho has become an important source of island revenue. Beneath a rainbow flag in the same portside travel agency the Lesbos Pride Tour Company advertised same-sex holiday activities. They were Gay and Lesbian Mezze Get-togethers. For more adventurous and sporty types there was Gay and Lesbian Donkey Trekking. And for those with a bent for pilgrimage there was always Eresos, the birthplace of Sappho herself.

A word of warning to anyone looking for a little

homoerotic diversion in sunny Greece: before packing a bag for Lesbos, think twice about gay and lesbian donkey trekking. It is awfully hot out there, even in the spring. I rented a motor-scooter in Molyvos and even with the highway breeze rushing by me all I could think of by noon was deep shade and cold water. As for nocturnal entertainment, consider other, possibly livelier places as well. Lesbian get-aways, like all other get-aways, fall into trendy and not-so-trendy categories. Molyvos was definitely in the latter group. It was a sort of family lesbian holiday place, if that makes sense. Many of the female couples sitting at restaurant tables in the evenings, German and Dutch for the most part, were middle-aged and had obviously co-habited a long time. An evening out with their partners was evidently about as exciting as shelling peas or assembling flat-pack furniture. They were barely looking at each other.

On the other hand, I did meet a young Greek woman who told me of a three-day lesbian festival held for the last few years in Molyvos in mid-summer. It seemed to have been hijacked by factional lesbian extremists. My Greek correspondent had lived most of her life in a Western European capital, only recently returning to the island her parents had emigrated from. She regarded herself as liberal and enlightened, but the festival disgusted her. I shall call her X, in light of her outspoken opposition to it and threats from antagonists that she'd have the crap kicked out of her if there was any more complaining. Our conversation took this kind of turn:

X: Same-sex sex doesn't generally upset me. But you would not believe the kind of women who showed up here. They were hardcore lesbian militants. They had tattoos and piercings everywhere. And I mean everywhere. That didn't bother me so much. But some of them had their skulls shaved. They wore combat fatigues and army boots. They weren't normal people – they were intimidating and physically aggressive.

Me: They sound like Nazi paratroopers.

X: They were worse. They were Nazi heterophobe paratroopers.

Me: But what harm could they do at a festival?

X: Festival? They wanted to hold what they called

an all-day Pussy Party. On the beach outside Molyvos. Three thousand fascist lesbians, unleashed in the full light of day! Is there no shame?

Me: God! A Pussy Party! What happens at a gathering like that?

X: I cannot possibly tell you. Unspeakable things.

Me: Go on, tell me – what happens?

X: No, I really can't, because the locals broke it up. It got very nasty. It caused a scandal here, and a scandal in western Europe. The press was full of headlines like 'Greeks Send Lesbians Packing', and 'Lesbians vs. Lesbians in Holiday Island Sex War.' It was horrible. Of course they want to stage it again this summer.

Me: Really? It sounds unmissable. Do you know the dates?

But the truth was that I was actually far more interested in the island itself than its invaders, either Turks or lesbians. In a few days I would be catching the little ferry that crossed the narrow straits between Lesbos and the town of Ayvalik in Turkey. From there

54

it wasn't far to Gallipoli and then on to Istanbul, a megalopolis whose estimated population is regularly revised upwards by a million or so. The last thing I wanted at the moment was crowds of any kind. So every morning I would hop on my motor-scooter, whiz out of town, and wind my way through a thousand bends to the prettiest, most deserted places I could find.

It wasn't hard on Lesbos. After Crete and Évvia it is the largest island in Greece. Parts of it were covered in hilly oak and pine forests. There were also vast swathes of olive groves, fields of wheat, flooded salt-pans full of birdlife, ranch-size stretches of cattle-land. The western half of the island was volcanic, a rugged near-desert, and ethereally beautiful. But in this season the whole island was fresh and inviting. Everything was alive with shifting light and colour, from the green olive trees that turned silvery-grey as I drove past, to fields of young wheat that streamed and rippled like waves in the breeze. Even the waste-ground by the side of the highway danced and fizzled, its swaying poppies tiny pinpoints of exploding colour.

Best of all was the coastline, steep and rocky almost everywhere. Riding through dazzling sunshine, I would roll along high over the sea. Calm and unruffled, the water changed colour as it ran away from the shore, turning from clear turquoise to opaque ultramarine. The sky, too, was made of graduated blues. Light and luminous at the horizon, it was as dark and deep as the sea itself by the time it was straight overhead. It was by the water, on the coast road running west to the beach at Sappho's Erressos, that I found one of the loveliest places on the island.

The unpaved track running down to Archea Antissa – Ancient Antissa – was steep and bumpy, and what lay at the end of it was so old there wasn't a great deal left. The first Aeolians to inhabit Lesbos arrived more than 3,000 years ago and built a colony on a small, narrow-necked headland here. It was difficult to see the remains close up, so I walked back along the shore to a stone church, from whose vantage point I could see ruined walls and towers.

There wasn't a soul about, but the door of the church was unlocked. Inside, sitting beneath framed

Byzantine prints and a wooden iconostasis, was a tray containing the accoutrements of an Orthodox service – candles, olive oil and a plate of aromatic incense. None of it was very formal. The candles, pink and with little plastic cups on their stems to catch the wax, were of the birthday-cake variety. They sat ready to be lit beside a Bic disposable lighter. The olive oil was kept in an old cough-medicine bottle. Short on ritual, the atmosphere in the church was all the more powerful for its simplicity, remoteness and silence. The only thing I could hear was a lapping of nearby waves.

Outside, I stripped off and slid into the water. It was cool and silky, and when I opened my eyes beneath the surface, clear enough to swim my way around rocks and weed-beds. I bathed for a long time and on emerging dried off in the sunshine. An onshore wind was picking up.

Even with my shoes back on I was afraid of snakes and scorpions in the tall weeds that grew in the ruins of Archea Antissa. Lizards sunned themselves on rocks and there were worrisome slithering noises as I climbed the hill that rose inside old, collapsed walls. But the wild fennel, tall and feathery, was so fragrant, the smell of the plants crushed beneath my feet so aromatic, that I kept climbing. And when I reached the top I found myself standing on a flat, grassy shelf with nothing between me and the water far beneath. I didn't know anything about the Greek Aeolians, apart from the fact that they traced their ancestry to the mythical Aeolus, god of the wind. But it seemed to me the open place where I stood was as much an altar as the one that lay in the church below.

Ahead, the sea was even livelier with light and colour than the land behind. Appearing as sudden patches of dark, fast-moving agitation, heavy gusts of wind tore across violet-coloured water. The Aegean might have looked empty, but it was full of an unseen, living force, one great breath after another sweeping over it to buffet the shore.

The wind kept growing in strength until it flattened the grass and was howling through the remains of crumbling walls. It was exhilarating and just a little bit frightening – I was alone, and yet not quite alone. In places like this it wasn't hard to believe that even now there might be something to those powerful old myths of gods and air-spirits. I left Lesbos a day later, wind-battered and content, having met the oldest island-occupiers of them all.

Four

There is an odd thing about the seawater that flows through those narrow and spectacular Turkish straits, the Bosphorus and the Dardanelles. To non-scientific landlubbers like me it seems wholly improbable, but it is a fact that the current between the Mediterranean and the Black Sea flows in both directions at the same time.

It is a piece of information of no conceivable personal use, but I find it fascinating. Apparently it has to do with salinity levels. Being an almost enclosed sea in a warm, sunny part of the world, the Mediterranean loses more water through evaporation than it gains through rainfall or the discharge of rivers. It is thus a good deal saltier than other seas, and getting saltier all the time. The water that replenishes it through narrow entrances is colder and much less salty – the Black Sea, especially, is fed by large amounts of fresh water from rivers like the Danube and the Don. Compared to the Mediterranean it is merely brackish. For reasons beyond my comprehension these waters don't easily mix. In the Dardanelles, as at Gibraltar, fresher water rushes into the Mediterranean along the surface of the narrow straits. Far underneath there is compensating movement in the opposite direction – heavier, denser, more saline water creeps along the bottom northward into the Black Sea. So different is the salinity between surface and deep-sea waters there that the two levels never mix at all. Only the top 500 feet of the Black Sea contains marine life – never oxygenated because it never comes to the surface, the 5,000 feet of water below contain no organic life whatsoever.

End of discourse on marine hydrology. And all that simply to say that when the bus from Ayvalik dropped down the steep hills towards the Dardanelles on a hot afternoon in early June I immediately felt refreshed. So lively and bracing was the cold water that flowed past Çanakkale, so revitalizing were the cool fingers of air wafting through the streets of the town that I, too, felt suddenly oxygenated. After a bus ride through a wavy, heat-bent countryside that announced the coming of a harsh summer, life on the banks of the Dardanelles felt suddenly fresh and bubbly. The air was clean, colours were bright, and out on the water a steady northerly breeze was kicking up small whitecaps.

Çanakkale, not surprisingly, is a navy town. For anyone who controls the strait here – at Çanakkale it is less than a mile wide – controls a good deal. Not only are these narrows the defensive approaches to Istanbul and the gateway between two inland seas; the Dardanelles are a strategic link between East and West as well. Time and again the place known to the classical Greeks as the Hellespont has been a focus of conflict. In the more poetic accounts Trojans and Achaeans may have battled over Helen, the most beautiful woman in the world. The real fight on these narrows, though, was over control of the Black Sea grain trade. Here King Xerxes built his bridge of boats across the Hellespont in the 5th century BC Persian invasion of Greece. It was here, too, that Ottoman Turks were ferried for the first time from Asia to Europe – they came not to invade Byzantium, but as mercenaries hired by the Byzantine Emperor John Cantacuzenus to help put down an internal rebellion. Small wonder, then, that the Turks have maintained a strong military presence here ever since – in the middle of Çanakkale looms the grim stone-walled fortress of Çimenlik, one of eight waterside fortifications guarding the Dardanelles.

I'd been drawn to Çimenlik by a passing-out parade of naval cadets. Their buttons gleaming, their dress-uniforms and shoes of a whiteness only naval officers seem capable of attaining, they had marched out of the Military Zone surrounding the fortress and down Çanakkale's main street. You could tell – the jubilant brass-band aside – that they were happy. There were smiles on boyish faces, an extra spring in their step, and rolled-up diplomas in each new junior officer's gloved left hand. After months of training in a Turkish military installation I think I'd be happy, too.

Çimenlik is still an active defence zone but it also houses a naval museum, and after the parade had marched out I marched in through the fortress gates. Scattered beside paths on precision-mown lawns were more torpedoes and cannons than anyone but an ordnance expert would care to see. But the paths led down to quays where clear, cold seawater flowed by at what seemed an alarming rate. I could hardly imagine Byron or any other Hellespont swimmer launching himself towards the other side. Even the *Nusrat*, a much-revered First World War minelayer, now lay protected from the current and permanently anchored in a small, still sea of concrete up on the quay. I toured her with a party of Turkish school-children until the exuberant clamour got to be too much. Jumping ship, I stood outside enjoying the water and watching commercial traffic make its way through the straits.

I asked a marine guard standing nearby if he could read the port of registration painted on the back of the *Milos*, a gigantic, bright red tanker now disap-pearing southwards. Soon it would be in the busy

Mediterranean shipping lane that the sooty, smoke-spewing *Rodanthi* had crossed on its way to Lesbos. But it was too far for his eyes also.

'How far away is it?' I asked.

'I will show you something,' said the guard, tipping back his sailor's cap. 'It is very useful, something every gunner knows.' His English was good; he said he'd learnt it on the internet. 'Hold your arm out to the Milos, raise your thumb and close one eye. Note the place you see behind your thumb. Now open your eye and close the other eye. Note this place too. Estimate the distance between the two places, multiply by ten, and that will give you the exact distance to your target. Try now.'

'Boom!' he said softly, going through the procedure with me, then lobbing an imaginary shell straight through the tanker's hull. 'What distance did you get?'

'A kilometre,' I said.

'No boom,' he said, looking crestfallen, as if an easy answer had unexpectedly evaded a star pupil. 'That ship is 1,700 metres away. You must practise.'

I took my rebuke silently, like a soldier. Knowing how to shell giant oil tankers seemed like another useless piece of information, but one never knew. I would keep at it.

'And what about that?' I said, swivelling my thumb towards the far side of the Dardanelles. There on a hillside stood the gigantic silhouette of an infantryman, hundreds of feet long and outlined in rocks painted white. Beside it, also traced in white rocks, were four lines of Turkish script.

'Oh, that is easy,' said the guard grinning, himself the star pupil now. 'It is not necessary to look; I know every word with my eyes closed.' And screwing his eyes shut he slowly, dramatically recited the verse, beginning *'Dur yocul! Bilmedin gelip bastığın.'* After Greek the intonations were strange, soft and guttural at the same time, and full of odd vowels and dipthongs that sounded as if they should have come from Scandinavia.

'And in English now,' he said, delighting in his display. 'Every tourist wants to know. I learned it from the *Lonely Planet*:

Traveller, halt! The soil you tread
Once witnessed the end of an era
Listen! In this quiet mound
There once beat the heart of a nation.

'Why is it in the *Lonely Planet?*' I asked.

'In Turkish the peninsula on the other side of the water is named Gelibolu. Every foreigner who comes here visits it. You call it Gallipoli. '

Towards evening I returned to my hotel. I had found it by following signs painted with an Australian flag and a legend that read:

Yellow Rose Pension
G'day Mate
Mr Ozal, Family Run.

And the Yellow Rose was indeed full of people who said 'G'day Mate'. Even the Ozals, big and little, talked like that. But by this point I was getting used to the accent. There were Australians everywhere – you heard them in the streets, in the restaurants, in cafés along the waterfront. But nowhere was Australianness more concentrated than in Anzac House, the teeming backpackers' hotel, restaurant and travel agency where I went that evening after dinner.

'Hey, Mate, what's the difference between a bison and a buffalo?' said the young Turkish clerk behind the desk. He didn't sound like a Turk. He sounded like he'd just surfed here from Bondi Beach.

'I don't know,' I said. 'Is there a difference?'

'Course there is, Mate!' he chimed. 'You ever tried washing your hands in a buffalo?'

Good on 'im – he must have cracked them up a thousand times with that one. But the Australians gathered at Anzac House hadn't come for the jokes. They'd come for the movies, and every evening for years it had been the same two. The first was an Australian documentary on the country's most famous engagement in the First World War. The second was more of the same in dramatic form – *Gallipoli* featured a young Mel Gibson, handsome and dashing in the uniform of the Australian Light Horse Brigade, heading straight into hell on earth.

I am not sure which film, emotionally speaking, the audience found more powerful – the solemn, measured tones of the documentary, or the sight of a naked Mel Gibson being shelled as he and his comrades tried to find a little relief from war with a swim on the beach beneath Turkish guns. But in the end the calamity of one of the First World War's bloodiest and most futile campaigns moved everyone in the audience. Of the 38,000 British Empire troops who died in nine months of trench warfare at Gallipoli 28,000 were British and 10,000 were Anzacs – soldiers of the Australia and New Zealand Army Corps. Fully half of the 500,000 Turks who fought there became casualties, and 55,000 were killed. For Australians though, it was a signal Australian event, a young country's baptism of fire. Going nowhere, achieving nothing, marked by poor planning and inept leadership, the campaign came to be seen as a tragic rite of passage from colony to nationhood. Eight thousand Australians were killed at Gallipoli. These days more than half as many again show up every year just to pay their respects.

After the films were over there was a flurry of T-shirt sales at the reception desk. The shirts showed a silhouette of Australian troops storming the heights of Gallipoli. Below was printed the second quatrain I'd seen that day. Banjo Paterson gave the same emotions a more popular cadence than his Turkish counterpart:

> *The mettle that a race can show*
> *is proved with shot and steel*
> *and now we know what nations know*
> *and feel what nations feel*

I was looking above the desk at signed photos of the Australian Cricket Board's Gallipoli visit when a voice behind me asked: 'Goin' on the Die Tour?'

God, I thought, they don't mince their words. 'Which tour is that?' I asked.

'Leaves here every die at nine o'clock,' said Cameron. Cameron was in his early twenties, wore baggy shorts and flip-flops, and had a large tin clutched in an even larger hand. He was a fan of Australian Rules football, a hanger-out at Brisbane beaches and an avid drinker of beer. Victoria Bitter being but a distant memory, he was doing his best to chill out with Turkish lager. It just didn't compare, he said. But when it came to patriotic pride beer brands faded into insignificance. Cameron was in Gallipoli to see where his great-grandfather had died fighting.

'Supposed to be a good tour,' he said. 'They throw in a late lunch, then run you up to Istanbul. You could probably get in a few cold ones along the way.'

Well, why not, I thought. Seeing Gallipoli is obviously best done in the company of Australians. So, like Mel Gibson, I signed up right away.

There were seven of us in the minibus the next morning. I'd never been on a battlefield tour before. I thought they were for older people, but none of these travellers was over thirty. It was a very casual, very Australian, very baggy-shorts-and-flip-flop kind of group. Just one man, Ali Efe, our guide, was middle-aged. His own grandfather had been killed at Gallipoli. He'd been a military man himself, a submarine commander before he'd retired, but his

72

authority was natural and easy and he got along well with his group. He smoked like a fiend. It made me wonder what it would be like to be submerged in a submarine in a tricky strait with a Turkish crew of heavy smokers anxious about water flowing two ways. It didn't bear imagining.

But neither did Lone Pine, the first battle-site we visited. 'Here,' said Ali, as we walked along the top of a steep escarpment, 'is the only place where ground was ever won or lost from fixed positions in the whole campaign. It totalled thirty-nine metres. Four thousand Turks and 2,000 Australians died in a space the size of two tennis courts. They are buried in common graves beneath us.'

The thought of 6,000 dead men strewn beneath out feet was enough to calm the two blondes who'd been cackling ferociously in the back of the minibus ever since we'd boarded the ferry at Çanakkale. Cath was a short-order cook in North London and Viv an Earl's Court barmaid. They'd been sharing a £160-a-week bed-sit in the year since they'd left Australia. They couldn't stomach anything about the English, they said – not their food, or their manners, or their cost of living. They put it all down to the weather.

'It rains all the time. It's cold,' said Cath.

'When you spend that much time indoors you can't help it,' said Viv. 'It's either Playstation or drugs.'

But, they had to admit, they were having the best time ever. They loved the London scene. They loved parties and new people and clubbing and being away from boring Sydney suburbs and not having to see their families and taking off to places like Turkey on cheap holidays. Cath and Viv were bubble-brained ditzes and they found it hard to stop talking for even a minute.

But now they pulled out the little bunches of flowers they'd prepared and placed them at the foot of the white stone monument in the middle of Lone Pine.

'Now don't start me crying, Viv,' Cath said. Viv didn't say a word but Cath started crying anyway. Cameron and his girlfriend wandered off down rows of headstones, looking for his great-grandfather's name. He didn't seem too organised and I didn't think he stood much chance of success — there are thirty-one war cemeteries on the Gallipoli peninsula. That left Ali Efe to cope with Terry, a fierce Melbourne republican whose hatred of war was almost as great as her hatred of authority — British authority, especially. While the others were content to listen to Ali and then stroll about, Terry would sniff around Ali's historical commentary like a dog on a scent — wherever she smelled the slightest whiff of opportunity she was straight into the fight. She loved to hear about the imperial upper classes treating the working-class colonials under their command as inferior expendables.

'Bloody Poms,' she'd mutter with a dark scowl, 'Incompetent, arrogant, supercilious, condescending fucking Poms.' Ali's account only confirmed what she already knew about the entire British race.

And so the morning drew on, the minibus dropping us at cemeteries, grassy fields, landing beaches and half-filled trenches lying only yards apart. Chunuk Bair, Shrapnel Valley, Anzac Cove, Jonston's Jolly ... each place was more murderous than the last.

'Three days were lost after the British landed divisions at Suvla Bay,' Ali would say, pointing down the coast to a beautiful curving sweep of blue water. 'They had to wait for artillery to arrive from Egypt. It gave the Turks time to dig in and prepare.'

'Bloody Poms,' Terry would growl.

'Yeh, bloody Pommies,' Cath and Viv would echo. They were delighted with Terry. Here was a new way to get back at shoddy public health services, underground train delays and £4.60-an-hour salaries.

'British High Command sent men to certain death in four successive suicidal attacks here,' Ali said as we stood at The Nek. 'The soldiers knew it and they went ahead anyway. They were very brave. The Turks called this place "the Hill of Courage" in honour of their enemy.'

'Ah, the Poms.'

'The bleeding Poms'

'Those Pommie fuckwits.'

Terry's resentment was infectious – there was now general stirring among the whole party whenever the British were mentioned. It struck me that if retired Commander Efe was doing a fair job repairing Australian-Turkish relations, he was doing a superlative one sabotaging ties between Australians and Englishmen.

But of his overall belief in man's humanity to man there could be no doubt. After years spent reciting the same sad story, Ali Efe still respected soldiers' bravery. What he revered even more, though, was their brotherhood.

'These were ordinary men, Turks and Australians, doing their duty,' he said as we sat in shade in the heat of midday. 'But after much killing and suffering the soldiers realized the ugliness of politicians. They hated war. They stopped killing each other. They realised that, whatever race, they were all human beings.'

I wasn't entirely convinced of the historical truth of what he was saying. If Gallipoli was finally evacuated it was in order that British and Commonwealth troops be thrown into the even bloodier battlefields of northern Europe.

'The suffering and loss here was great,' Ali went

on, 'but in the end both sides gained something. The Turks gained Atatürk, who became famous at Gallipoli as a fearless general and leader of men. Without him we would be like Iran or Saudi Arabia today. And the Australians gained the Anzac spirit, the birth of their belief in themselves. Not long ago Turks and Australians thought each other the most dangerous people on earth.' He searched for a symbol of compatibility. 'Now we mix together like sardines in a basket.'

And here Ali performed his own small commemoration ceremony, presenting each of us with a spent bullet dug from the earth of Gallipoli. We all applauded him. Cath and Viv enjoyed the presentation so much they began crying again.

An hour later we had eaten lunch at a restaurant beside the straits and were waiting for the bus to take us north. Cameron had not found his great-grandfather's grave, but he didn't seem upset.

'No worries,' he said, draining yet another beer. 'I wouldn't have missed it for anything. Great Grand-dad's not feeling any pain. Christ, but it's hot, isn't it? Do you think we could get some cold tinnies for the ride?'

We did, and so arrived six hours later in Istanbul, not feeling too much pain either.

Five

It was midnight by the time the bus rolled off the Marmara coast highway and into Sultanahmet, the heart of the city. It wasn't late for Istanbul, but it was late for a tired and wobbly traveller unused to the beer-quaffing style of Australian Rules. I tried consulting the Sultanahmet map in my guidebook, but in the bus's dim lighting I could barely make out Aya Sofya and the Blue Mosque, much less the dozens of small hotels marked in surrounding side-streets. Instead I looked through the window and watched the minarets above the mosque, slender, brightly illuminated rockets aimed into the black night. They grew closer and higher. When they were near enough to be an easy walk, I got the driver to let me down and made my way to the first hotel I saw. Twenty minutes later I was asleep.

The Onur was not a grand hotel. It was a gangly hotel instead. Tall and thin, sandwiched into a row of other skinny buildings, its seventeen beds were distributed, two rooms to a floor, over five stories. The rooms were narrow. The stairways were steep. The shower-stalls were slim. But when I woke in the morning and stumped up to the rooftop terrace for breakfast I was delighted with the Onur's gawkiness. Rising above surrounding buildings, it not only looked up a steep hillside to the dome and pencil minarets of the Blue Mosque. Downhill, it looked out over the Sea of Marmara and busy shipping funnelling past Seraglio Point into the throat of the Bosphorus. From the Onur Hotel all Istanbul appeared thin and attenuated.

All, that is, but Yilmaz, the hotel's proprietor. He was dark and bristly, a stocky, thick-set Kurd from Bingöl in eastern Anatolia. He looked like a country labourer, but in fact there was nothing rural about him. When he offered me an omelette it was with an accent that had the inflections of both England and America. Yilmaz had worked in the hotel business in Bath. He'd lived in New Jersey. He knew the United

States better than I did – he'd made a living there towing a U-Haul trailer. He'd followed the motorcycle festival circuit from Orlando to San Francisco and from his stand sold black leather jackets, belts, chaps, studded wrist-straps and other fancy bikers' gear. He had, as you might expect, a breezy, confident air about him – you couldn't get away with less when you sold contemporary tribal-wear to Hell's Angels. Village Turkey lay a long way behind him.

Stirring sugar into a little tulip-shaped glass of tea, I was looking over the water at a dozen freighters riding at anchor when we were joined by a couple of hotel residents. They, too, had a breezy, relaxed air. They were so familiar with the place that they paid no attention to the sack-shaped, headscarfed cook in the kitchen on the floor below, but proceeded to rustle up their own breakfast. John and Jan had already been at the hotel for a few weeks, and were likely to stay on for several more. They were broke. They did their own shopping and cooked meals in the hotel kitchen. They commandeered the reception desk computer to write e-mails to their families. They scrounged cigarettes from the proprietor. They brought homey domesticity to the Onur Hotel.

'We're just like family,' said John, putting his arm around Yilmaz's shoulder as Jan set down a tray. Yilmaz grinned munificently. He had given John and Jan his lowest, extra-special discount rate.

John was American and his wife Thai. In his mid-thirties, John had a candid, open face and the unguarded ways of the Midwesterner abroad. But he had bailed out of conventional American life long ago. Not even the peripheral existence he had tried in Alaska and Hawaii had been far enough removed. He had left it all behind to study Mahayana Buddhism in Singapore. He had moved on to Hinhayana Buddhism in Taiwan. He had meditated outdoors under an umbrella for three months. He had undergone cures by traditional Chinese medicine. In Thailand he had met Jan and taken over a patch of her parents' hill-farm. It still wasn't enough. John wanted to get even further away from civilisation and all its works.

He and Jan had decided to travel the earth's biggest oceans, crewing their way around the world on other people's yachts until they could raise money to buy their own. As we sat on our rooftop perch, eating toast and watching ships sail into the Bosphorus, John told me about their sea voyage from Thailand – the plank-springing, Hong Kong-built wooden boat they had joined; its eccentric German owner and smelly, menacing Gypsy crewman, Giuseppe; the horrendous storms off Sri Lanka; their reception by hostile Muslim fundamentalists on the Sudanese coast; the venality of corrupt Red Sea customs officials; the decision, taken in Port Said, to abandon the boat before it sank beneath them. Now John and Jan were marooned in Istanbul, hard-up and biding their time until the late summer sailing season when they could find a boat to crew on from the Azores across the Atlantic to the Caribbean.

If John and Jan's confidence in the peaceful serenity of life at sea had been tested to the limit they remained committed to their new life. It was liberation for them. For Yilmaz, on the other hand, the life John had run from in despair was *his* liberation. He loved America and its opportunities. John would talk about the jungle farm in Thailand, encounters with Muslim Sufis in remote, forgotten seaports, the spiritually bankrupt state of the modern Western world. Yilmaz would respond with observations from another life, a world in which neon-lit roadside bars, all-night driving marathons and wild blonde biker-chicks figured large. The biker-chicks, especially – and the kinds of thing they're capable of when they meet truly hunky Kurds out on the blacktop wilderness of the Interstate highway – were a Yilmaz leitmotif. It was wacky dialogue, *On the Road* meets *Walden*.

'That's crazy and impossible,' Yilmaz would chuckle dismissively at some utopian world-vision of John's.

'That's immoral and disgusting,' John would react to Yilmaz's account of an especially depraved road-trip.

But each enjoyed the other's fascination with opposing cultures – it was the reason Yilmaz gave the couple a room practically free of charge. And I enjoyed it too. These were the kind of conversational exchanges that are only easily sustained in big, cosmopolitan cities like Istanbul, the meeting-places of the world.

So on my first day in Istanbul I, too, was contemplating settling down semi-permanently in the Onur Hotel. But around lunch-time a telephone call home to Aix-en-Provence changed everything. Being married to a teacher of languages had its benefits. Once again Jany's continent-wide network of contacts had kicked into life. Through her own cosmopolitan encounters Jany had met a teacher, who knew another teacher, who had a colleague who'd been seconded to work in a French-language *lycée* in Istanbul. The links connecting these individuals, a thin thread running eastwards from France to the edge of Asia, were tenuous. But they led to an irresistible destination – the oldest foreign school in Istanbul, established in a labyrinthine Jesuit monastery under Ottoman rule in the 16th century. Barring Topkapi Palace and a few other imperial piles, there was barely a more venerable address in the whole city to put up at. It would take a little arranging, but in a couple of days there would be a room available for me there. In the meantime I had the Onur, and the old quarter of Sultanahmet around it to explore.

In fact I didn't make it any further that day than a carpet shop up the road. John and Jan didn't have the money to run around town doing the things visitors to Istanbul usually do. Most days they spent time with yet other Turkish Kurds they had met, four cousins who ran a family business selling carpets from their home villages in eastern Anatolia. They invited me to the shop in a busy tourist area off the Hippodrome.

Hakan, the shop's owner, didn't appear terribly trustworthy to me – his smile was wide and his hand went over his heart in a gesture of welcome, but his look was slippery. None of his three 'cousins', slick and ingratiating young men in leather jackets, looked any too honest either. They put too much emphasis on their simple country origins, were too effusive in their vows of hospitality to strangers. They offered us cigarettes, brought cushions and sat us down in the midst of a spotlit showroom piled high with sumptuous fabrics. To me Hakan and his associates looked like carpet conmen.

But they had befriended John and Jan, entertained them, pressed food and drink upon them, made protestations of eternal friendship. Their relatives, they'd promised, would soon receive them in their humble peasant homes in the hills. The couple could stay and be fed as long as they liked, and not a single Turkish lira would change hands in return. It all put John, morally correct as ever, under a sense of inescapable obligation. But lately he'd been troubled – his friends weren't turning out quite the simple, stalwart villagers they claimed to be.

'I'm not sure they are 100 per cent honest,' John whispered to me when the Kurds went off to a back-room to prepare tea. 'First I discovered they're not really cousins at all. And I suspect one of them is a sort of stool pigeon – I think he sells information to the police. Another flies every couple of weeks to Amsterdam with large amounts of cash – I saw it in a suitcase before he went to the airport. And the third, I'm pretty sure, has a part-time career as an enforcer – I think he beats people up for money.'

Wanting to believe the best of everyone, John had

to admit before mounting evidence that his friends might not be entirely virtuous. In the meantime he was doing his best to repay their hospitality by helping to sell carpets.

It was Hakan who had suggested it. When it came to Western tourists John was his front-man. With his innocent face and easy conversation, John could persuade any number of potential customers off the street and into the shop where Hakan sat like a waiting spider. Their defences lowered, their trust and confidence raised, passers-by were suitably softened up even before they got into the master's hands. And once there, few walked away unscathed.

The talent of the Istanbul carpet salesman is a wonder to behold. It is an ancient art combining a dozen disciplines. It entails the subtlest skills of communication. It calls on the greatest technical expertise. It requires assertion and insistence, flattery and compromise. It demands elegance, manners, and split-second timing. In its finest form it is a game of moral suasion – it depends on the seller obtaining psychological advantage over the buyer, drawing him by a dozen unseen tricks into a corner from which there is no way out. In the end, short of bringing his own honesty and goodwill into question, the customer becomes ethically bound to buy an object he was never really sure he wanted in the first place.

No doubt there are principled sellers and happy buyers of carpets. Neither was in evidence in Hakan's carpet shop. I watched four sales that afternoon, complex rituals of carpets thrown lavishly, one after another, at the feet of unsuspecting visitors – they ranged from a wealthy South African couple inveigled in minutes into buying a $6,000 silk prayer rug, to a British student backpacker who agonised for an hour over a bright and nasty $35 kilim. All of them, though, walked out scratching their heads in wonder.

How, they asked themselves, had this happened? How had they been strolling along the street one moment, and the next signing American Express travellers' cheques? Hakan, of course, knew the answer. It happened because John – consumer-society renegade, seeker of truth, student of the Eight-fold Path and the Middle Way – had helped them buy it.

Early that evening, a tidy profit realised, Hakan, John and the rest of us sat down cross-legged on a carpet to a small, well-earned feast. There were crisply grilled sardines, olives, slices of cucumber, crusty bread, and plenty of chilled beer and raki. The company was loud and merry – everyone was in a good mood.

I had arrived in Istanbul at street level, I thought – the meeting between East and West doesn't get any more basic than this. Hakan and his so-called cousins were rogues, but cheerful rogues, and I didn't like them any the less for selling over-priced carpets to tourists on holiday. It was certainly a better way of making a living than beating up people who failed to pay their debts on time. Nor did I like John any less for assisting them – this was globalisation, too, the way one part of the world becomes familiar with another. Given the right circumstances John might even make a carpet seller himself, but an ethical one, and help bring decency and good practice to the trade.

In the meantime there was food and talk and wild

Kurdish singing, a soulful lament for a distant, lost way of life. It was very late in the evening by the time we made our way back to the Onur.

ISTANBUL

Six

I woke up in doubt the next morning. Where was I to begin, carpet shops aside, in a place like Istanbul?

This was not one city, but many. For more than 1,500 years it had been the dazzling capital of two successive empires. It had been a political and administrative hub, a religious centre, a military stronghold and the greatest commercial and trading emporium in the world. It was Greek Byzantium. It was Constantinoupolis Nea Roma, the new Roman empire of Constantine and capital of eastern Christendom. It was Konstantiniyye, the centre of a Muslim Ottoman empire that had stretched from Baghdad to Budapest. And now it was Istanbul, the most varied, sophisticated and outward-looking city in modern Turkey. It was a port on the threshold of the Mediterranean. It was also an Eastern city and a Western city, European and Asian, imperial and republican, traditional and modernist, secular and religious. To ancient Byzantines it was the navel of the world, the place at which all things converged. To today's Istanbuliots it was still that, a galloping, unstoppable city twenty miles deep and a hundred miles wide, a megalopolis that refused to cease growing.

Where to start? Difficult as the question was, I only had to look out from the Onur's rooftop to know the answer.

Twenty-seven hundred years ago a Greek named Byzas, about to set off to found a colony on the Bosphorus, approached the oracle at Delphi and asked where precisely he should site it.

The oracle, so the story goes, answered, 'Opposite the blind', an answer that at the time mystified the colonists. But when Byzas and his fellow settlers sailed up the Bosphorus, they came across another Greek colony at Chalcedon, now Kadiköy, on the Asian side of the narrows. Gazing to the European side of the strait directly opposite, they saw that marvellous deep-water anchorage, the seven-mile-long Golden Horn. It wasn't hard for Byzas to decide that the citizens of Chalcedon must indeed be blind to ignore such a site. So at that place he founded Byzantium. The city began with the sea, and so would I.

It takes just fifteen minutes to walk from the tourist crowds swirling around the Blue Mosque to the still thicker commuter crowds swamping the Eminönü ferry quays on the Golden Horn. But as I walked down to the Horn the next morning neither tourists nor commuters were spending any more time than necessary strolling outdoors. Bad weather had blown in overnight – heavy with low, scudding cloud, the skies over Istanbul brought one squall after another sweeping across the city.

The weather wasn't enough, though, to discourage the Bosphorus ferry passengers making the day-trip up to the Black Sea and back. Joining a crowd of excursionists on a rain-soaked quay I couldn't help thinking of another sopping waterfront far to the west – for a moment I was back again in rainy spring weather on the Grand Canal in Venice. From the ferry's covered stern the city that rose beyond the quays resembled Venice all the more.

It was precisely the same dull colour. Everything blended soggily into everything else. The stone of the mosques, the walls of the spice markets, the old weathered roofs of merchant's warehouses – all matched the dirty grey wash of the sky. On the road running along the waterfront broad puddles were pocked with rain and the air was full of the sound of bus tyres hissing their way over slick black tarmac. Behind me on the Galata Bridge, men fishing in the Golden Horn wore water-streaked rain jackets and plastic bags pulled onto their heads. Pouring dark and intent off arriving ferries, Istanbul office-goers, just like Venetian office-goers, leaned their bodies and their umbrellas into the wet, gusty wind.

It wasn't just the rain that made the two cities seem alike. Nor was it the architecture, the random, vertical scattering of mosque and minaret that so resembled that of church dome and campanile. It wasn't even the general wateriness of the place – the prospect of flat, wet surfaces, silvery and rain-pitted, that ran away into the distance. It was none of these things alone. What made Istanbul and Venice similar was their liquid energy, the exuberant, exhilarating, endlessly-changing spectacle of life borne upon water. Both cities had the same relentless aquatic drive.

Wherever you looked there were boats – not leisure boats for sitting and resting, but busy boats for living and working. The coming and going of Bosphorus ferries, large, double-decked steel vessels spouting sudden palls of grimy smoke, was ceaseless. They arrived from Üsküdar and Haydarpaşa on the Asian side, from up the narrows at Beşiktas and Bebek and Yeniköy, from the Prince's Islands off in the Marmara Sea, with a hurried self-importance that was barely polite. Moored at deep-water quays at Karaköy on the other side of the Horn, ocean-going ships of the Turkish Maritime Lines were also preparing to leave – to the Aegean and Ionian, to the Adriatic and to other Mediterranean seas beyond. Ukrainian cruise-liners lay waiting to sail for the Black Sea. From landings near the Galata Bridge local water-taxis, as battered and humble as Venetian water-taxis were snooty, industriously chugged their way inland along the inner edges of the Horn. In the other direction small rowboats skittered like water-insects about the mouth of the Horn, their occupants pulling lustily on oars or jigging hand-lines from seats in the stern.

Even the little boat tied to the quay directly below me was busy. It wasn't going anywhere except up and down, a violent rocking in the surging wake of departing ferries. But with its open charcoal fire and hot, pan-swirling oil, it was voyage enough. Braced against constant pitching and tossing, raincoated and baseball-capped against blustery weather, its adventurous crew, cooks to a man, were settling down to another day of making the finest fried-mackerel sandwiches in Istanbul.

Soon the engines beneath me were thrown into gear, the foot-worn planking of the wooden deck juddered, and my ferry, too, was in motion. Quickly the noise of honking traffic on the Galata Bridge faded and the yellow slickers of fishermen grew faint. The tall, stone-built Galata Tower, a construction that would have looked more at home in Renaissance north Italy than here in Istanbul, slid by on one side. The pleasure-palaces and kiosks of Topkapi eased past on the other. And then the confines of the Golden Horn were behind us. Quitting the ferry terminal at Eminönü is a bit like exiting Santa Lucia railway station in Venice – suddenly the Bosphorus opens up before you like a wide, restless highway, and you are on the grandest of Grand Canals.

It is only when the passenger pulls away from the shore and looks back from mid-stream in the Bosphorus that the full magnificence of the port-city becomes apparent. From out there I could see a narrowing, hilly promontory pointing from the European side of the strait towards Asia. On its southern edge began the broad Sea of Marmara, on its northern flank the deep-water inlet of the Golden Horn. Along with the Bosphorus itself, these bodies of water surrounded Istanbul on three sides. They had long made the city a natural fortress. Nor were its narrow land-approaches any less well defended – for a thousand years they'd been protected by the most splendid stone walls ever built. Even in the 19th century, when the barrier raised by the Emperor Theodosius was crumbling and inhabited by goats and greenery, Byron enthused that in all his travels through the classical world he had never beheld a work of nature or art quite as imposing. Few cities have so often been the object of men's envy, or so successfully withstood their attacks. Nor, on the only two occasions when Constantinople actually was overwhelmed – the Venetian sack of 1204 and the Ottoman conquest in 1453 – was the destiny of the Mediterranean world so radically altered.

Human history may move in sudden, unpredictable lurches, but the progress of the ferryboat was stately and relentless. There was no time to think of the past. Istanbul dropped behind. Like Venetian palazzi on that other canal, successive waterside scenes now began looming left and right as the ferry threaded its way up the Bosphorus. Even in rain and drifting fog they delighted the passengers. Everything along the banks – parks, pavilions, fishing ports, fortresses, forests, palaces, villas and villages – seemed to have found its perfect natural setting. Admirals of the world's navies could talk about the strategic importance of the Bosphorus. Maritime shippers could praise its commercial benefits. Geologists could discuss its tectonic functions, geographers its role as a divider of continents, climates and cultures. But we ordinary mortals immediately knew the Bosphorus for what it was above and beyond all those things: the loveliest, most enchanting sea-passage on the face of the globe.

Parties of foreigners from every corner of the world skipped across the decks of the ferry, from port to starboard and back again as the whim took them. There was an itinerant, fleet-footed assembly of Korean ladies, all in identical orange jackets, determined to photograph each other in front of every sight along the way. There were solemn families of Malaysian Muslims, the boys in embroidered skullcaps, the little girls wearing ankle-length coats and scarves tied beneath their chins. A festive group of Brazilians chattered their way up the Bosphorus. A cluster of French tourists, glancing repeatedly up and down in concerned, Cartesian manner, worried over their map and questioned its placement of Bosphorus sites. Hardy in shorts, socks and sandals, a pack of leathery Germans lunched on sandwiches pulled from rucksacks. Navigating between these groups were Turkish waiters elegant in white shirts and black ties. They kept their flashing smiles for the younger foreign female passengers, but briskly plied us all with glasses of steaming tea and little tubs of fresh yoghurt.

Proffered a plastic spoon, I ended up sampling some from a tub bought by a California couple.

'Matt always reads up before he goes anywhere,' said Susan, Matt's wife. 'The yoghurt on the Bosphorus ferries comes from Kanlica, a town on the Asian side famous for its high-quality milk and dairy products.'

Her husband was probably right – it was pretty good yoghurt. If Matt went in for thorough briefings before he did anything on his holidays it was only because he stuck to the professional habits of a lifetime. Fair-haired, healthy and youthful, Matt had recently retired from a flying career. He'd begun jockeying American jet-fighters over south-east Asia and ended up piloting Airbuses across the Atlantic. Now he and Susan flew free of charge to holiday destinations around the world.

'What Matt didn't plan for was the weather,' said Susan. 'It's not supposed to be raining.' She seemed surprised Matt hadn't got Turkish meteorology better in hand. 'Tomorrow we're going yachting – we've chartered a boat for a week on the Turkish Mediterranean coast. Things don't look too good.'

Perhaps that was why Matt kept sweeping the horizon to the south with his binoculars – he was looking for a break in the weather. But all he kept sighting were Turkish navy ships.

'Destroyer,' he would say, passing me the glasses. 'See how her silhouette masses up high to the tower in the middle? You can't mistake a destroyer even at twenty miles.'

'Matt flew from an aircraft carrier in the South China Sea,' said Susan. 'In fact, he holds the record for the longest single aerial-combat engagement in the whole Vietnam War.'

'Yeah, but I wasn't alone,' said Matt. 'There were

six F-4s against twelve MiGs. And it might have seemed to go on forever, but the whole thing lasted less than five minutes. Time gets sort of elastic up there.'

And so the morning and the world floated by. We looked at mine-sweepers and torpedo boats through Matt's binoculars. At Dolmabahçe and Beylerbeyi we cruised past imperial Ottoman palaces, sprawling 19th-century wedding cakes of marble. We slipped by waterside *yali*s, lovely fret-worked wooden houses once favoured by viziers and princesses, today the pride of Turkish millionaires and industrialists. We passed under the Bosphorus and Fatih Bridges, spans of flying steel and cable so high that the trucks and buses above us looked like toys. Beneath the first bridge a giant hanging banner of blue and yellow, the colours of the city's Fenerbahçe Football Club, swirled and fluttered in the rain.

At Kanlica Pier the socked-and-sandaled Germans disembarked beneath the dismissive gaze of even tougher, more resiliant Turks – in a cold wind they were fishing from the dock in rolled-up shirtsleeves.

At Yeniköy all the Malaysians descended. At Sariyer the Korean ladies disappeared. But we stayed on, fighting a fast current as tankers and tugs, container-loaded freighters and camouflaged submarine-chasers swept down past us. We finally got down at Anadolu Kavagi, the turn-around point where the Bosphorus widens to meet the Black Sea. We had a couple of hours to wait before the return journey.

We tramped up to the Byzantine-built fortress above the village, Matt and Susan holding umbrellas aloft against a steady drizzle, our feet slipping in mud by the roadside. The fortress of Anadolu Kavagi wasn't much to see in drifting mist. It wasn't much to see anyway. Sodden dogs, their coats stained dark by rain, had knocked over refuse bins in the picnic grounds outside the high stone walls and spread garbage far and wide. Inside, little toilet-paper-covered mounds in the corners beneath defensive towers discouraged further exploration. It was cold and windy, and only in a fish restaurant back down at the port did we warm up again.

The food wasn't wonderful. It didn't have to be;

in good weather hundreds of ferryboat tourists pass through the fish restaurants of Anadolu Kavagi every day, never to return. But the wine was cheering and it was good to be dry again – we felt cosy sitting in front of a big picture window upstairs watching fishing boats bob in the little harbour in front of us. Just beyond them, big ships moved at speed in the narrow shipping lanes.

The sight woke a memory in Matt's mind. He began talking about an accident at sea – the running-over of several Vietnamese fishing junks by the aircraft carrier he'd flown from during the war.

'We smashed into them like so much driftwood,' he said, looking at the brightly painted boats, their decks covered with nets and orange buoys. 'They fell into a thousand pieces.'

'Why didn't you just go around?' said Susan. 'You must have seen them.'

'Sure we saw them,' he replied. 'But you can't turn a 900-foot ship on a blowy day in the middle of a flight operation. Planes have to launch and land into the wind. So we ran them over.'

It sounded callous. I wondered if Susan had heard the story before and asked the next question to make it sound less callous. 'Did you pick up survivors afterwards?' she asked.

'Yeah, I guess we eventually picked them up and dried them off,' said Matt.

'Did you buy them new fishing boats? Did you kill any of them, drown them?' Perhaps Susan hadn't heard the story.

Matt only shrugged. We stopped talking about aircraft carriers, and a few minutes later heard the ferry horn hoot passengers back on board for the return journey.

Halfway down the Bosphorus again, at the foot of the Fatih Bridge, we passed Rumeli Hisar, the Fortress of Europe. On the way up we'd been gazing skyward at the bridge and hardly noticed it. But now here the fortress was, its rough walls running down uneven banks to the water, its stone towers looking wild and medieval beneath the smooth steel risers of the bridge. Long after Rumeli Hisar disappeared past our stern I was still thinking of it – behind its construction lay a violent meeting of two ways of life quite as different as American capitalism and Asian communism were to be 500 years later.

The fortress had been raised in record time by the Ottoman Sultan Mehmet II, otherwise known as 'el-Fatih', the Conqueror. So anxious was he to take Greek Constantinople, the city both his father and great-grandfather had besieged, that he had it thrown up in a mere four months. In 1452 he ordered each of his three Viziers to take responsibility for one of the fortress's three main towers – failure to complete them on time, the story runs, would have resulted in their execution. And when the Fortress of Europe was finished, Mehmet used it to block off this narrowest point of the Bosphorus – no longer could Constantinople be provisioned from the north by the sea.

Less than a year later, in 1453, his armies besieged the city walls. Two hundred and fifty years after its sack by Venetians and Crusaders, Constantinople was a mere shadow of itself. It possessed few of its former territories. Its population had shrunk from 400,000 to less than 50,000 – the once-great city was now a straggling collection of half-abandoned parishes separated by fields and pastures. Its monuments had been stripped, its wonders sold or stolen. Even the lead on the roof of Hagia Sofia, the 900-year-old church of Divine Wisdom, had been melted to mint coins. The only surprise was that the city had held on as long as it did.

Moribund, living on borrowed time, its 5,000 fighting men facing an army of 300,000, Constantinople put up great resistance by land and sea. Even its monks fought. In the end the city's conquest was aided by a vast gun, a taste of Ottoman military superiority to come. A novel weapon whose first testing had terrified peasants and caused women to faint, it was twenty-eight feet long, fired a half-tonne cannonball for a mile and required a special carriage drawn by thirty oxen to haul it. The millennium-old walls of Constantinople were not designed for cannon. It had about the same effect on them as an aircraft carrier on a fishing junk.

Cannon at that time were relatively new on the field of conquest, and so were the Ottomans. When

ISTANBUL
XI 2002

Mehmet II entered the city on a white horse through streets being put to bloody sack, he dismounted before Hagia Sofia, swept up a handful of earth and poured it over his turban. It was intended as a show of humility before God. But he and his ancestors had never displayed the same humility before men – their lurch to power had been proud and sudden.

The Ottomans, later such proficient saltwater sailors, had come riding out of the arid steppes of central Asia in the 1100s. Even there, rootless pastoral nomads, they'd seen themselves as chosen, a people of destiny. They were pulled westward by a better climate and the failing power of the Byzantine Empire. By the early 1300s the soldiers of Osman, the first in a dynastic line of Sultans, had reached the Marmara shores.

If military success followed fast and furiously, a lot had to do with Ottoman encouragement of Muslim *gazis*, combatants anxious to fight in holy wars against Christians. Such conflict brought great virtue, and even greater booty. By the mid-1300s the Ottoman capital had moved from Anatolia to

Edirne on the European side of the Bosphorus. In the following decades Ottomans swept not just through Anatolia, but Bulgaria, Serbia and much of the rest of the Balkans as well. By the time Mehmet the Conqueror stood before the walls of Constantinople it was nothing more than a tiny island in an already wide Ottoman sea.

To the Ottomans, intoxicated by success, it appeared only right that the greatest city in the world should be theirs. It seemed tailor-made, a city shaped by geography and history to be the capital of world rulers. Constantinople commanded sea-lanes to the Mediterranean, Africa and the Black Sea. It lay on overland trade routes between Asia, the Near East and Europe. Nowhere else on earth seemed quite as central, as perfectly situated for the imperial domination of the four quarters of the globe. Constantinople's ambit was religious, too. In the city where Hagia Sofia was transformed into the great Ottoman mosque of Aya Sofya, the Caliphate – the world-centre of Islamic rule – installed itself and there remained until modern times.

I was so immersed in contemplating changes to the ancient city that I missed a change taking place immediately around us. It was hardly historical, but it put a smile on Matt's face.

'Check it out,' he said, passing me the binoculars and pointing southwards. I did, and towards the Sea of Marmara saw open spaces between the clouds, and beyond them clear sky. By the time we were nudging into the ferry-quay at Eminönü the sky had cleared still further. A late afternoon sun was now out, and I understood for the first time why they called it the Golden Horn. As far down the inlet's surface as I could see, the water and every human being near it was lit by a warm, bouncing glow of reflected light. Before turning back to Sultanahmet and home, I walked out to the middle of the Galata Bridge just to stand in the Horn's glittering reflection.

Anyone could see why Mehmet, and every other strongman before or since, had wanted this city.

Seven

A couple of days later I was back on the Galata Bridge. This time, my bag over my shoulder, I crossed its entire length and kept on going.

I climbed through a warren of streets rising steeply away from the water on the far side, puffing my way past busy artisans' workshops and the premises of minor traders. Halfway up the hill, where stray dogs slept sprawled about a small park at the foot of the Galata Tower, I turned onto a residential side-street. Three large Turkish women, sitting on front door steps in long, flowered dresses, watched idly as I dropped my bag before a gate sunk into a high wall. I fished in my pocket for the ring of heavy brass keys Madame Annie had given me. I was at the rear entrance of my new lodgings, the Lycée Saint-Benoît.

You had to go a long way back, almost to the beginnings of Galata itself, to find the origins of Saint-Benoît. If the hillside above the Golden Horn is still a quarter of traders and small-time commerce, it has been so for more than a thousand years. In Byzantine times a community of foreign merchants – Genoese principally, but also Venetians, Florentines and other Western Europeans – grew up opposite walled Constantinople. The Franks flourished on the East-West commerce that placed the city at the very heart of things. Perhaps not feeling entirely protected by the trade agreements they had signed with the emperor – Byzantines did not have duplicitous reputations for nothing – they raised their own walls, erected the tall stone defensive tower that still stands there, and proceeded to build warehouses, churches and homes. In Galata they created what was virtually a small north-Italian city, and inside closed communities lived prosperous lives according to their own ways.

There was little resemblance to the great eastern city that lay just across the Horn, and that difference remained remarkable throughout Ottoman rule as well. Today Galata and the wealthier and even more westernised quarter of Pera on the hilltop behind it are called Beyoglu – son of the *bey*, or lord – after one of its best-known 16th-century residents. Excluded by his illegitimacy from any suitable career in Venice, Alvise Gritti, bastard son of the Doge Andrea Gritti, settled in Galata instead. He'd been born there – as a young man Andrea Gritti had been a Galata merchant and fathered Alvise by an Ottoman concubine. There the son of the lord dealt in jewels and acted as a diplomatic agent for the Sultan's Grand Vizier. Like thousands of other westerners over the centuries, he not only made a fortune in Constantinople but became a go-between for two cultures. He was also famous for his lavish entertainments, inviting Turkish nobles to huge banquets and treating them to displays by Galata's notorious dancing girls, specialists, as one knowledgeable observer noted, in 'such lascivious movements that they could make marbles melt'.

For general wantonness and debauchery Galata's countless taverns and brothels remained celebrated among the world's sailors right into the 20th century.

But the community's more genteel residents were catered for as well. Among Franciscan, Cistercian and other religious orders, there were Benedictine clerics from the great French abbey of Cluny serving on the Bosphorus even before the Frank's sack of Constantinople. But when in 1204 the Latin invaders took control of the city's 12,000 Greek Orthodox churches and 300 monasteries, efforts to draw them into the Roman fold brought new waves of monkish orders to the city. They built their own churches, too. In the mid-1300s the Republic of Genoa, Venice's great trading rival in the East, was renovating the Galata Tower and expanding city walls; at the same time it also undertook to pay for a new church and monastery to be built by Benedictines just below the tower. This was the institution through whose creaking back gate I now let myself.

I barely knew my way around. I had only gotten my keys from Madame Annie, the school secretary, after meeting Saint-Benoît's principal the day before. Now it was a Saturday and there wasn't a soul around to ask directions. With a large key I opened a heavy wooden door into a main building, swung it closed behind me, then plunged forward through near-obscurity down a high, echoing hallway.

The place soon had me spooked. The only light came from windows lying beyond open classroom doors on either side of the hall. Each time I poked my head into one of these rooms I would be met by the same cold gaze – since the early years of the republic a portrait of Kemal Atatürk has hung in every classroom in Turkey. His eyes were piercing, his gaze cold and forbidding. He made the old building feel more ghost-ridden than a hundred monastery crucifixes could.

It was like a bad dream – the dark hallways went on and on, turning left and right but never leading anywhere. Once I found myself in a dusty storeroom piled high with books centuries old, their ancient leather binding disintegrating, their Greek and Latin print shot through with wormholes. Once I encountered a ceiling-high display case, the pelicans, storks and other large stuffed birds inside it fixing me with beady glass eyes as I passed. I negotiated a series of interior courtyards and several sets of gloomy

121

stairwells. I tried other floors that turned out to be just as confusing as the ones above and below. After twenty minutes of rising panic, I at last found the locked metal door I was looking for.

Sitting beneath high antique beams, the air-conditioned guest accommodation that lay beyond was opulent for any school. The armchairs were deep, the hardwood floors polished, the lighting soft and indirect. There was a wide-screen television the size of a small car. Not far from a stone fireplace, rising unexpectedly out of the floor and protected by heavy glass, was the complex spring-and-cog mechanism of a 19th-century clock. On its frosted glass face, incorporated into the wall and overlooking the school quadrangle on the other side of it, I could read, letters inverted, the words 'Collin, Paris'.

In the 500 years since Saint-Benoît had opened a school for the children of Galata Catholics it had not always been as prosperous. Fishing for Catholic converts amongst the Sultan's Orthodox subjects was hardly a wise public relations gambit. There had been worse. In the 16th century the monastery's

Brother Joseph de Léonisse, charged with seeing to the spiritual salvation of the Sultan's Catholic galley slaves, was so inspired by them that he impulsively sought an audience with the Sultan himself and called on him to embrace Christianity immediately. Restrictions on Catholic monks were tightened and Brother Joseph, for all his effrontery, merely thrown into prison – he might have ended up with his head impaled on the walls of the first courtyard of Topkapi Palace.

Benedictines, Dominicans, Jesuits – and finally, after the French Revolution, French Lazarists – administered the monastery. All knew uncertain times. Often short of funding from home, the Lazarists were obliged to raise revenues locally. They published a Turkish grammar in French. They established an Armenian language press. They even cultivated a commercial jasmine plantation in the monastery courtyards. And their diligence paid off – today the Lazarists still run Saint-Benoît. Their prosperity is assured by the fees paid by the wealthy parents of their Turkish students. And if they are prohibited from inculcating any kind of faith in their charges, their secular teachers turn out the next-best thing to Turkish Catholics – Turks instructed in the ways of the French. *La Mission Civilatrice* continues.

It certainly continued in the suite of rooms I had been assigned on the far side of the spring-and-cog clock. It was entirely civilised, its furnishings pleasing from both Eastern and Western points of view. In my study I discovered a 19th-century print of the Bosphorus at sunset. Entitled '*Palais du Sultan et Bateau de Parade*', it showed the Sultan arriving at Dolmabahçe Palace in his royal *caique*. Long and narrow, its high prow carved and gilded, the vessel was powered by thirteen pairs of rowers dressed in red fezzes, white uniforms and black waistbands. Lounging beneath a richly-decorated canopy at the stern, his chin bearded and his turban feathered, an imperial potentate took his leisure. It was a scene of pomp and ceremonial splendour, and it looked all too familiar – here was an eastern Doge sitting before an Ottoman Ducal Palace in an oriental state-vessel. Sea-sovereigns never change.

But maybe in the end they have to. In the bedroom beyond I came across a second, very different picture. It, too, was a waterscape, and also 19th century. But it was a blown-up, panoramic photograph of the Golden Horn and it showed another Istanbul. It had none of the first picture's Oriental decadence – this was a vista of industrial-age transport, an image of funnelled steamships, smoky skies and the new, floating steel-pontoon Galata Bridge. The ships were massed side by side and the bridge jammed with pedestrians in a hurry. You could almost hear the bellowing of porters, the klaxon of horse-drawn trams, the chattering of telegraph lines. All Western energy and vigour, Constantinople was no less frantic than the ports of New York or London at the time.

And this was what had made the port-city so extraordinary – the fact that *caique* and steamship existed alongside each other at the same time. Saint-Benoît was an early example of attempts to bring European ideas to an Asian metropolis. But it was only one initiative in a long process in which East and West met and mingled in Constantinople, and in many cases fused.

Neither side, of course, was fired by mere altruism. As elsewhere around the globe, France's civilising mission was never lacking in self-interest. In Constantinople France found an ally against her European arch-rival, Spain. And when in the late 1600s long-successful Ottoman institutions began failing an empire that had outgrown them, a reverse process set in – the Ottomans began looking westward for their own advantage.

Their empire needed modernisation and France, at the forefront in great-power relations with Turkey, was only too happy to oblige. Like other nations of the European Concert during the age of nationalism, she was poised in a delicate balance of power – each country, afraid that Turkey and its imperial possessions might fall into the hands of the others, cooperated in a collective effort to prop up the famously 'sick man of Europe'. Who could have put it more candidly than the Duke of Wellington? 'The Ottoman Empire stands not for the benefit of the Turks,' he pronounced, 'but of Christian Europe.' Without European assistance it would have fallen far sooner than it did.

From battle tactics to ballet techniques, the French were everywhere in the effort to reform and westernise the ailing power. They taught modern artillery to its armies, European construction to its engineers, Western surgery to its doctors, continental administration to its bureaucrats and French poetry to its students; by the end of the 1800s more than 5,000 French words had become Ottoman words. But a Gallicised elite was not enough to help the Ottomans survive – in the end Western knowledge came too little and too late to allow them to adapt to a fast-changing world.

Today the French still delight in instruction, but now, it seemed to me, they came to Istanbul to learn just as much as to teach. Soon after settling into Saint-Benoît I was invited to a party in the suburb of Bebek, halfway up the Bosphorus. Normally I think I would have hesitated over an evening hosted by a *professeur de mathematiques* for a group of science teachers. But Farida and her guests were about as unconventional as French *lycée* instructors can get.

I took a taxi to the soirée early one evening with

Florent, the Saint-Benoît teacher who'd arranged my rooms at the old monastery. Florent taught information technology, and after a year in Istanbul he had no desire to return to the same job in France. In fact he had no desire to return to France at all. He was learning Turkish, a hard slog in a tongue that resembles no Indo-European language whatsoever. He played the *darbuka*, a Turkish drum, and rather than spend his holidays in France went trekking in remote mountain ranges in Anatolia. He had fallen in love with Turkish carpets. Florent was going native, as far as that is possible in a city that in some measure has been European from the beginning.

It was the same with the other foreigners there. The taxi skirted the edge of the Bosphorus and just before the Bebek ferry pier, in an affluent suburb between the strait's two bridges, climbed upwards to a house poised high over the water. Tables and chairs had been set up under fruit trees in the garden outside. The plums there were still hard and green, but the cherries were ripe and red and began to glisten in the light of the candles flickering beneath them.

From the edge of the garden you could see freighters churning their way up the Bosphorus – they were so close you could almost spit cherry pits at them. Who could blame the French gathered in the garden at sunset for not wanting to leave the city? They had fallen in love with Istanbul, and made of their lives in it a happy mix of East and West. All of them told me the same thing. With their Turkish friends there was a directness of engagement, an ease and comfort in daily human contact they hadn't known before. Was it perhaps a holdover belonging to what was left of an older, more cohesive society? At any rate it gave them a sense of complicity that had long ago been swallowed up by modern French life.

And what of Farida, Saint-Benoît's young and pretty mathematics teacher? She had a natural warmth, a level, curious gaze, and an immediate sincereity, even with strangers, that was disarming. But beneath the candour there was a tough, uncompromising resilience. She had made some hard choices.

Farida was light-skinned and clear-eyed, a Berber born in a remote town of the Middle Atlas mountains in Morocco. Her grandfather had been a traditional hill-chief, an adamant, unbending tribal elder with a strong religious bent. He had trained his son to be a Muslim imam, but Farida's father had fled the town's poverty – and its overbearing patriarch – choosing instead the life of a migrant labourer in France. Farida had arrived there as a baby.

Farida's younger sister Naïma was born in France, and had chosen the more extreme option available to those cut off from their roots – religious reaction. In some ways she was a modern, professional woman – she worked in the marketing division of a French car-manufacturer. But she had also taken the Islamic headscarf and lived the conspicuous life of a devout Muslim. Growing up in the same high-rise, low-income immigrant suburb outside Paris, Farida had gone a different route. She'd studied hydro-electric engineering.

'I wanted a modern, liberated life. I wanted freedom and equality,' she told me as the night drew on and we watched Florent light a charcoal grill. 'And I couldn't find it in France. I was the Muslim fundamentalist's sister, the Arab factory-worker's daughter who had found her way up and out. I'd become a proper Frenchwoman. But I didn't want to be a social phenomenon – I wanted to be myself.'

She'd sought escape in rural village life in southern France, looking for neighbours, human ties, close-knit community. 'I realised later,' she said, 'that what I was looking for were the same connections, the same kind of social fabric I might find in a more traditional life – in Berber life, for example. It doesn't exist in France any more. So I moved again. I came to Turkey.'

And did she find those connections in the sprawling, modern megalopolis of Istanbul, I asked? Farida shook her head.

'No. But I've found a kind of mental space in which at least I feel comfortable. Turks have the same doubts I do – they feel divided about religion and secularism. They're unsure about being both Western and Eastern.' She laughed. 'So I'm a fish in water here. Teaching school maths isn't what I imagined for myself and it won't last forever. In the meantime I can cope with all the questions and still get on with life.'

Was this the Mediterranean at work again, that inter-connective, cosmopolitan influence that blurred origins, that made for a wider sense of identity? In Alexandria I had found the last remaining traces of that kind of society, but it was close to dying. Was it still possible, even today in Istanbul, to share in more than one identity? It was dark now and the grill had burned down to a red glow. More guests arrived – other French and their Turkish friends, couples who lived neither European nor Oriental lives, but both.

We dined on tabouli and grilled lamb and Turkish wine. After there was dancing. I stood on the parapet watching the lights of ships describing slow, broad curves through the dark straits – if a few stars burned faintly in the clear sky above, entire bright constellations of lights were passing by on the decks of giant tankers below. Every now and then a ship's horn gave a long, loud blast and an echo would reverberate up the hillside to the dancers on the lawn.

And so we sat by the Bosphorus, refugees all, listening to ships and drinking wine into the night. Later the music and dancing stopped, people began drifting home, and finally there was only the sound of Florent softly playing his *darbuka*. I sat with Farida, sometimes talking, sometimes thinking about her group of friends. What was the lure that attracted such people to Istanbul? I left an hour before dawn, and by the time a taxi dropped me at the foot of the Galata Tower there was light to the east over the water.

Eight

I tried to get a feel for the capital of the Ottomans through its most famous monuments, but it wasn't much good. If there are a dozen buses parked outside it doesn't matter which place you're visiting – inside it's always the same place.

Istanbul was not far now from the full-blown summer tourist season and the palaces, mosques and jewelled treasure-collections of Sultanahmet were overrun. I have nothing against such visitors. There is no reason why a couple of dozen excursionists from, say, the Göteborg branch of the Swedish Association of Dental Hygienists should not admire the Iznik tile-work of the Blue Mosque. I have even less against the hawkers who make their living selling trinkets in the street. Is there any denying that the world of

Swedish dental care would be a happier place if only its practitioners brought home a few embroidered caps with swinging tassles? What wrecks everything is when twenty or thirty such tourist groups descend on one place and attract entire marauding bands of street-hawkers. It all becomes pointless noise and confusion. In the midst of it the fainter voices you've come to listen for simply slip away, back into the past.

So it was with relief that I came to the end of several rounds of intensive sightseeing. My one real satisfaction had been in seeing the tomb of the Venetian Doge Enrico Dandolo, who died in Constantinople after overseeing its sack, left forgotten and ignored in an obscure corner of the Aya Sofya. I finished up just down the road with Istanbul's most popular tourist-scramble. Why exactly the Sultan's harem in the heart of the Topkapi Palace should have such drawing-power was a mystery. Did the crowds surging around the ticket office in the third courtyard think they were buying admission to heaven on earth? Were they surprised to discover there were no Circassian slave-girls with alabaster skin and perfumed thighs reclining in the cramped little rooms at the top of narrow palace stairs? The chambers were hardly redolent of seduction – the press of flesh the tourists themselves produced there was merely sweaty and clamorous. Duty done, I took myself off to quieter, calmer places.

I spent a day strolling beneath the sixty-foot height of the city's Byzantine walls. There were no tourists milling below the wall's ruined Tekfur Palace. It was a remote part of the city – the only hygienists were bus drivers who used the waste-ground there as a place to wash their buses. Borrowing a ladder from one of them, I scaled a break in the palace fortifications, climbed to the roof of a tower and gazed down onto an old field of battle. Tranquil now, it wasn't hard to repopulate it with a massed and heaving army of Ottoman soldiers – it wasn't far from here that after seven weeks of siege Mehmet the Conqueror's Janissary troops had breached the city walls and entered Constantinople.

I spent another day walking the narrow streets of Fener and Balat, quiet quarters a couple of miles up the

Golden Horn. Most old residential areas of Istanbul disappeared long ago, their wooden houses victims of modern property development and the great fires that regularly used to sweep the city. But these areas, traditionally the homes of Ottoman ethnic minorities – Balat is Jewish and Fener Greek – remain poor and largely undeveloped. Dodging kids playing ball in the street, I walked into an earlier century. Crooked stovepipes protruded from the sides of sagging and ramshackle wooden houses. Hanging laundry swayed in the breeze. Shady vines sprouted in tiny gardens and ran up trellises over the street. It was quintessentially Mediterranean – this could have been backstreet Naples, a hillside in Marseilles or a waterfront quarter of Tunis. But here I didn't have to strain at all to catch the voices of the past – in Balat an elderly man approached and addressed me in Ladino, the Spanish dialect that has been used by Jews in Constantinople since their eviction from Spain 500 years ago. We just about managed.

There were scores of old places like these, peaceful and uncrowded, scattered all over Istanbul. One of my favourites I discovered on an airless, sultry afternoon when the heat of the streets had become too much. What I craved was a bit of freshness and greenery, and I found it in Ihlamur Kasri, the Kiosk of the Linden Tree, preferred retreat of the 19th-century Sultan Abdulmecid.

The entrance ticket I bought at the gate to Ihlamur included a guided visit of the Sultan's kiosks. But as I was the only visitor around and the custodian on duty was a sociable type with nothing else to do, the tour was downgraded – it turned into a leisurely stroll around the grounds with plenty of conversation thrown in for free.

The park was charming, a jewel hidden amidst concrete apartment blocks and growling traffic. I was led over crunching gravel paths through well-kept rose gardens, over manicured lawns and past a stone-lipped pool where carved lions sat looking at their reflections. We walked on through a less formal, hillier part of the grounds, where fragrant stands of linden, magnolia and pine trees gave us deep shade. The custodian, a large, paunchy man in a grey uniform and peaked cap, enjoyed the cool as much as I did – beneath his visor his face was florid and overheated. He didn't look Turkish at all. His hair, light brown, would have been straw-blond in his childhood. His eyes were an icy, penetrating blue. His name, like the Conqueror's, was Mehmet. And if he looked more like a Hungarian or a Pole than he did a Turk, he had definite views on his countrymen's past and their origins.

'Where you think the Turks came from?' Mehmet asked me conversationally as he stopped to mop his face. I could see he was going to tell me no matter what I replied, so I shrugged.

'A long time ago,' he said, walking on, 'there were two brothers. They lived by the water at Çanakkale. One was named Turka, and the other Franka. Each wanted to be a big man. They wanted land, a lot of money and many, many women. So they decided to go in different directions. Turka went east into Anatolia. Franka went west to France.'

I blinked, never having heard a folk-tale of Turkish beginnings before, and said nothing.

'They were the first Turks,' Mehmet said. 'Who do

you think the Kurds, the Armenians, the Egyptians, the Syrians and all the other people of the empire were? They came later, they were the Sultans' conquests.

'Franka was very handsome, with blue eyes and yellow hair. He had many pleasures with ladies,' Mehmet continued, giving me a man-of-the-world wink. 'And he made many children as he went west. Most Turks came from Romania, Albania, Kosovo, Bulgaria, Greece. This is God's truth. They were top-quality, number-one people. Original people! This is why the French are good people, too. Their ancestor is Franca. This is why they are strong and clever. This is why they are good soldiers. Napoleon, you must know, was a Turk.'

Here I couldn't help interrupting. 'Are you sure about that? The French say he was a Corsican.'

Mehmet was having none of it. 'No, no!' he insisted. 'Intelligent men, professors from big universities, have looked at this question, and decided it is so. There are many books on it, thick books.' He held up his hand, his thumb and index finger as far apart as possible.

The books I'd read weren't thick and hadn't said anything about two brothers, but I couldn't help getting Mehmet's point. Never mind all those dark and foreign-looking Eastern people, he was saying – we Turks are really much more European than Oriental. And for a blue-eyed Turk with a job looking after a building that was beyond all doubt European it was, in the end, an understandable point of view.

We had looped through the woods back towards civilisation. By the side of the path delicate wrought-iron lampposts now appeared. Discreetly equipped with hi-fi speakers painted forest-green, they were emitting the dulcet strains of a Mozart string quartet. The stands of wood thinned, the lawns grew broad again, and soon we were in front of the Kiosk of the Linden Tree. Who, standing before Abdulmecid's sylvan getaway, could doubt that Turka's brother Franka had made it not just to the Balkans, but all the way to the far end of the continent? Whoever had ordered up this stone-carved fantasy surely had to have had a little Gallic blood in his veins.

The kiosk was a French folly, an impossibly

romantic mix of baroque and Second Empire neo-classical architecture. A pleasure-pavilion wrought in marble, it dripped ornamentation – it was heavily loaded with half-columns, Corinthian capitals, urns, medallions, acanthus leaves, floral decorations, scalloped shells and bas-relief pyramids of fruit. It looked like a crazed pâtissier had squeezed it all out of an especially extravagant piping set. It was delicious and ready to eat.

The interior decorator had done himself no less proud. The salons inside – you simply couldn't call them rooms – were lavished with every European refinement. The vast chandelier was of Bohemian crystal. The vases were Sèvres. The Louis Seize chairs were upholstered with fine brocade. The coal-grated fireplace was enameled and covered with detailed floral decoration. Almost as much gold-leaf as glass, there was a gilded Hall of Mirrors that would not have shamed Versailles. Only the Imperial Water Closet featured recognisably eastern, squat-down design, but you couldn't accuse the Sultan of scrimping – at the time there wasn't a Western-style lavatory between

143

London and Vienna that would have met his approval. If his toilets were not elevated, the Sultan's standards were.

With a triumphant, I-told-you-so sort of smile on his face, Memed left me to ponder his interpretation of the Turkish past. Once again history, that inevitable companion of any traveller in the Middle East, had caught up with me and I was going to have to try to sort it out. I sat down on the edge of the stone-carved pool and gave myself up to the luxury of the surroundings and the warmth of the afternoon.

Mehmet's past was a past reduced to myth, but what he was saying wasn't all that wild. The story of two ambitious brothers riding out in opposite directions from the edge of the Bosphorus was no less expansionist than that much better-known Ottoman myth, the Islamic conquest of the Red Apple.

For the Ottomans the Red Apple, a metaphor for world domination, was originally the city of Constantinople. It was said to stand for the globe once grasped in the hand of a giant statue of the Emperor Justinian outside the Hagia Sophia. 'We shall meet at the Red

Apple,' generations of Ottoman sultans declared ceremonially to their Janissary generals as they assumed the reins of power, arming themselves with that other symbol, the sword of their ancestor Osman. But as the sword did its work and their dominion expanded, so the Red Apple changed – it remained a goal lying always just out of reach. For early Sultans sitting in the newly-built Topkapi Palace the Red Apple was the original western Christian capital, Rome. It later transformed itself into Vienna. Beyezid, son of Mehmet the Conqueror, confidently expected to move on past Vienna to Paris itself. What remained constant was the idea of continual military advance until war had subsumed the entire world into a single Ottoman commonwealth.

Nor, I thought, was Mehmet the Custodian wrong about the imperial enterprise being largely European, at least in its leadership. The Ottomans were never a nation, as the Turks were later to become. Issued from Muslim Turkish clans, they were a hereditary dynasty ruling over an empire in which Turks were just one component – to the elites of Ottoman culture

'Turk' was a disparaging term applied to unwashed Anatolian farmers. Not even the old Turkish clan nobility was enlisted as a base of support – it was seen as potentially troublesome. Instead, the Sultan's rule depended on the service of a foreign-born military and administrative class. Known as *kapi kulu*, Slaves of the Gate, such men were precisely that: imperial subjects whose lives from an early age belonged exclusively to the Palace. The 'Gate' referred to Topkapi's Cannon Gate, where the Sultan's justice was dispensed; it later evolved into the symbol of government known as the Sublime Porte. But the Slaves of the Gate were never Turks. Because the Koran forbid the enslavement of born Muslims, the Ottomans had to look further afield for each new generation of servants. Recruits came from Christian Europe.

It was a system that worked supremely well for almost 400 years. In Greece, Albania, Serbia, Bulgaria, Romania – any place in the Balkans that the Ottomans had recently conquered – a 'boy tribute' was levied on the rural Christian population. Converted to Islam in Constantinople, the

146

youths were placed where they would best serve the Empire. The brightest were given intensive educations at the Palace or under a Pasha's supervision. The best of them would eventually rise to the highest levels of administration – of the first forty-eight Grand Viziers heading Ottoman governments after the conquest of Constantinople, just eighteen were native-born Turks. Other boys were destined to become Janissaries, the Empire's elite corps of fighting men. Numbering some 20,000 they, too, were highly trained and held crucial positions of power. Their zealous and unflagging service was one of the secrets of the Ottomans' astounding military advances. But when as a sign of dissatisfaction the Janissary regiments overturned their pilaf cauldrons, the Sultans themselves trembled.

Ottoman 'slavery' is not entirely translatable, and the term did not carry the same significance it does in the West. The Sultan himself, after all, was the son of a slave, often one of those alabaster-skinned Circassians so favored in the harem. For a Slave of the Gate submission to empire meant escape from a life of rural Balkan poverty and ignorance. Becoming, in effect, members of a privileged extended family of which the Sultan was patriarch, the *kapi kulu*, sons of peasants, left the restrictions of feudalism behind. Subject to a rigorous process of selection, trained to the limits of their aptitudes, they entered a meritocracy in which intelligence, ability and loyalty were valued above all else.

Thus the children of mountain shepherds became viziers exalted above all ordinary men. Such opportunity, a direct contradiction of the principles of entrenched power and privilege sanctioned in the West, produced great motivation. It also, quite naturally, horrified Europe's medieval aristocracy. It proved that the much-vaunted virtues of hereditary nobility were a nonsense. Here was a system, wholly dismissive of feudal conventions, which in feeding off its triumphs was capable of advancing ever outwards. In the same way that the latest conquest provided the spoils of war necessary to fund the next military campaign, so too did it provide the personnel who would go on to execute the following stages of expansion. *Kapi kulu* could not pass on their slave status to their Muslim-born children, but as long as conquest was possible new recruits were available. Until it began to unravel the system provided the empire with an unending supply of warriors and administrators. Efficient and self-perpetuating, it gave the empire both dynamism and stability for centuries.

Seen by anyone standing in its way, the Ottoman empire was a formidable machine harnessed for endless conflict. Not for nothing were the lands outside its jurisdiction known as the *Dar al-Harb* – the Abode of War. But viewed from inside it was called something else: *Dar al-Islam* – the Abode of Peace. Unlike many other imperial conquerors, the Ottomans had no interest in forcibly making the peoples under their rule become like themselves. No one was commanded to speak Turkish or Ottoman Turk, the language of the elite. No one had to renounce the customs and habits of centuries. No one had to convert; eventually the promised Mahdi would come and put the world of the infidel to rights. In the meantime the Ottomans had themselves and an empire to maintain.

What they needed were not Muslims. They wanted taxpayers instead, and non-Muslims paid top rate.

And so from the beginning the *millet* – that method of multinational management which even much later cast its afterglow on 20th-century Alexandria – was a convenient and natural way to rule. It wasn't simply a matter of ensuring revenues. When the Sultan recognised any group's religious and ethnic identity he undertook to protect it and guaranteed its right to look after its own affairs. In return, however, he demanded every *millet*'s absolute loyalty to the empire; the principles of collective responsibility accepted by each community's leaders meant it was they, and not the Sultanate, who undertook to keep unruly internal factions in line.

I watched as Mehmet returned to the kiosk with a mixed party of visitors – Germans, Italians, and some Eastern Europeans. Not everyone understood Mehmet's English explanations, and he was having a tough time keeping the bored ones from wandering off on their own. It made me think of the problems history's great imperial rulers must have had in imposing order on their varied possessions. The practical advantages of the *millet* system of administration in a vast empire had been enormous. Mobile as they were, Ottoman armies could not march off at the drop of a hat to police distant corners of huge and mountainous territories. And as they grew larger the Ottomans' holdings grew infinitely more complex. Multicultural Alexandria was only a dim reflection of a far greater intricacy. Vlachs, Laz, Tartars, Bogomils, Bedouins, Serbs, Uzbeks ... at its height the Empire was said to be composed of seventy-two-and-a-half nationalities, the half-nationality being composed of Gypsies. In such a complex world, interconnected but self-contained communities made the only sense. Here were the origins of a cosmopolitan society unlike any in the West.

Attracting talent and ambition from every part of the empire, Constantinople became the heart of this interdependency, the only multinational capital in Europe. And its diverse and contrasting ways of life became the essence of the city. When Mehmet the Conqueror came on the scene the majority of his subjects, not just in the city but in the empire as a whole, were Christian. Anxious to repopulate and restore the metropolis to its former glory, he immediately set about attracting merchants, artists and craftsmen from all over. Some were Muslim Turks, some Jews, some Christians – Greeks, Armenians, Slavs and Levantines. He also reinstated a Greek Patriarchate, a religious body which had overseen Orthodox affairs from Constantinople since the 4th century. It was the beginning of a process of reciprocal bargaining, persuasion, threats, cajoling and political horse-trading which was to characterise ethnic relations inside the Empire until its very end.

Even at the best of times there were strains and tensions. Not all elements in Ottoman society were in favor of a multicultural ideal – from the beginning the *ulema*, the empire's community of Islamic theologians, professors and practitioners of Koranic law, often opposed the privileges accorded non-Muslim minorities. But the Ottomans' great gamble, that an ethnically disparate collection of peoples would function better under co-option than suppression, generally paid off. And for centuries Constantinople, the meeting place of many worlds, enjoyed a truly cosmopolitan existence. In the same way the Sultans combined European and Islamic and Ottoman identities in their own person, so was it possible for their subjects to have dual or even multiple identities. A Constantinopolite could be a Greek Jew, a Syrian Christian or a Hungarian Muslim. At the same time, however, he could feel still himself thoroughly Ottoman.

Why did cosmopolitanism stop working? Why did the Ottoman system of multicultural co-existence fall to pieces? Why was blue-eyed Mehmet now the grey-uniformed guardian of a superannuated pleasure-park when a distant forbear, resplendent in red boots and white linen hat, might have stood at the head of a battalion of triumphant Janissaries? For an answer I only had to look up from the rippled reflections in the pool to the extravagant building that lay beyond it.

Western Europe had had its own power and glory at the same time, too. And if its various states were fractious and quarrelsome, disputes between them had given the continent a combative vigor. In the centuries-old contest between East and West Europe had developed something that was wholly anathema to its Ottoman rivals – nationalism. As a creed it had become successful and attractive from Portugal to the Ottoman frontiers. By the mid-1800s even Venice, once the proudest and most independent of city-republics, had opted for union with Italy. Faced with the fervor of nations held together by patriotic myth – the vision of people of a single blood united in defense of a single language, history and sacred soil – the cosmopolitan ideal of a state based on plural cultural identity became a fast-fading irrelevance.

But in fact the Ottomans had built anachronism into their empire from the very beginning, and it began showing itself long before the age of nationalism reached such heights. The multi-ethnic state worked superbly from the 1300s through the 1500s, when the reign of Suleiman the Magnificent saw unparalleled successes in conquest and the consolidation of empire. Perhaps he was too successful. By the

154

end of his rule a major sea-change, barely perceptible at first, began to set in. The empire was reaching its natural limits.

If Ottoman power was based on an economy and labour market driven by war, then continuing conquest was essential. But there came a time when logistics alone began to make successful conquest more and more difficult. With an empire now stretching from Algiers to the Don River, from Budapest to the Persian Gulf, the Ottoman armies could no longer race like lightning as they once had across the confines of the Balkans; simply getting to the peripheries of their territory inside a single campaign season became a challenge. Warfare became a much slower and more exhausting activity.

Once the Ottoman armies had seemed unstoppable; with the war against Austria at the end of the 1500s the Ottomans' outward expansion finally and painfully creaked to a halt. In the peace accords that followed, the Sultan had to recognise his rival, the Austrian emperor, as an equal. Never before in Ottoman history had such a humbling admission been made. Even more of a climb-down, the Red Apple, the tantalising goal always just beyond reach on the far horizon, now slipped from view forever. World dominion, the ambition that had fuelled Ottoman confidence for so long, was now just an historical mirage.

There were crucial material consequences, too. There was less and less booty to pay the salaries of the vast Ottoman armies and bureaucracy. Inflation was rampant. Taxes became unbearable. With budgets and stipends wearing thin, bribery and the selling of office became widespread. Out in distant provinces venal and self-serving officials brought misgovernment and misery to new lows. Resentment and violence grew correspondingly. Failing in their multicultural ideal, the Ottomans provoked their own virulent, home-grown form of nationalism.

Inevitably, the Empire was sucked into its own downward spiral. Its sense of direction was lost, its people abused, its institutions riddled with sloth and corruption. Only when it was too late did its conservative elite begin to look to technological and political change as a means of shoring things up. I only had to look at the little pleasure-pavilion before me to see that there had been aspects of brilliance in the Ottoman's long, slow decline. But an ornate façade did little to prevent the final collapse of the Ottoman house. In many parts of the eastern Mediterranean they are still trying to clear away the resulting mess of political rubble today.

It was late afternoon and beginning to cool off by the time I rose from the pool. The same Mozart piece had wafted out over the lawns a dozen times now. I gave Mehmet a wave goodbye as I walked out of Ihlamur's gates. But he was too busy to notice – he was accompanying a newly-arrived French couple and I imagine he was explaining to them why Europeans were really Turks. I have no idea how they received the news about Napoleon.

Nine

Not far up the hill from where I stayed, on the other side of the Galata Tower, began the street called Istiklal Cadessi. I started going that way more and more because it was the opposite of everything I had seen so far — it wasn't Istanbul's past, but its future.

It didn't seem to matter what time of day I let myself out of the rear entrance of Saint-Benoît — the large ladies were almost always there, sitting barefoot on their doorsteps or on a carpet spread out on the sidewalk. I don't think I ever saw them without spoons in their hands. Either they were feeding numerous small children, or helping themselves from a communal bowl placed in the middle of the carpet. They were stolid, heavy women, prematurely aged by childbearing and domestic labour. They weren't beautiful, but their long, voluminous dresses were. The curlicue vines and tiny coloured flowers printed on the dresses' jet-black background were so bright they jumped out at you. Walking past these women was like walking through rural Anatolia, a place, presumably, they'd come from not long before. We never exchanged words, or even glances. Talking to strange men wasn't part of rural Anatolian protocol.

The dogs in the little park at the foot of the tower were always there, too. There are stories of dogs ruling the streets in the old days of Istanbul, large packs of howling, semi-wild brutes each controlling their own quarter and fed by a population who both feared and loved them. The half-dozen dogs I passed were big and rough-coated and still lived on handouts, but they didn't look as troublesome as they once might have – most of the time they simply blocked the sidewalks as they lay snoozing in the sunshine.

The steep street that led upwards from the tower specialised in Turkish music. Its shops were filled with delicate and exotic-looking string-instruments

– *baglamas* and *tamburs*, *kanuns* and *ouds* – and up and down its sidewalks odd, exotic sounds floated out into the air. The street attracted musicians from outside the quarter, but it still had an intimate, almost village-like feel to it. At its foot you might meet a horse-drawn cart offering piled watermelons for sale, or carrying dense little forests of fragrant potted basil plants. Higher up, on gradients too steep for any animal, you'd come across a handcart heading the other way. The man in front of it would be leaning far back in the cart's shafts, pushing hard with his shoulders as he struggled to ease the load gently down the hill.

And then, abruptly, the ascent would be over, the hill from the Golden Horn finally scaled. Broad and level, Istiklal Cadessi began its unhindered procession along the hill's crest towards Taksim Square, the heart of modern Istanbul. Gone were the anachronisms of an older world, the quaint scenes imported from dusty towns on faraway plains. There was no place for them on Istiklal Cadessi, the busiest, most sophisticated pedestrian thoroughfare in the entire eastern Mediterranean.

These days it is filled with the kind of establishment you'd find in any modern downtown shopping area: clothing boutiques and sports shops, restaurants and multiplex cinemas, bookshops and cash distributors and ice cream stands. A century ago the street had aspirations to much higher levels of fashion. Known as the Grande rue de Pera, it self-consciously styled itself on the great boulevards of 19th-century Paris. Pera matrons frequented shops like Bon Marché and La Maison des Modes Françaises. Pera husbands frequented brothels graced by grand stairways, wigged and powdered manservants and courtesans reclining on divans of red velvet. Together, husbands and wives frequented Taksim Gardens, a sort of Levantine Tivoli at the far end of the Grande rue; there they could sample the pleasures of a restaurant, an open-air cinema, a variety theatre, a cabaret and – as breathlessly described at the time in a local paper – a *bar ultra-select frequenté par le high life de la capitale*. Separated only by a quarter-mile of water from the still cramped, unlit streets of the oriental city across the Horn, the district was a modern marvel.

162

Like the population of Alexandria, the 180,000 residents of Pera living under the protection of foreign embassies had come to make money through trade. Like the Alexandrians, they too profited from tax and tariff exemptions, part of the Ottoman system of international 'Capitulations' granted from the 15th century onwards. And so from a very early date the capital was populated not just by the empire's many *millets*, but by numerous communities from beyond its borders as well. By 1718 Lady Mary Wortley Montagu, wife of the British ambassador to Constantinople, could write that 'in Péra they speak Turkish, Greek, Hebrew, Armenian, Slavonian, Wallachian, German, Dutch, French, English, Italian, Hungarian; and what is worse, there is ten of these languages spoke in my own family. My grooms are Arabs, my footmen, French, English and German, my Nurse an Armenian, my housemaids Russians, half a dozen other servants Greeks; my steward an Italian; my Janissaries Turks.'

Today the foreigners, like their languages and their footmen, have gone. But any number of European churches remain on Istiklal Cadessi, as do palatial former embassies. Brave efforts are also made by the few restaurants and hotels surviving from the turn of the last century. Not far off the street lies the Pera Palace Hotel, once Istanbul's finest. It is now a little less fine, perhaps a touch musty even, but nonetheless dear to wistful admirers of a privileged age of travel. No. 411, the room in which Agatha Christie is supposed to have written *Murder on the Orient Express*, has become a small museum. There are other establishments in the quarter, aging, washed-up remnants of that great tidal wave of White Russians fleeing revolution, where you can still get caviar, ice-cold vodka and a decent bowl of borscht.

But such places, it must be said, have become marginal curiosities, kept alive by travel writers drumming up nostalgia for Sunday papers. If a hundred years ago these institutions brought a vital Western energy to an Eastern city otherwise failing and moribund, things are different now. The present generators of Istiklal Cadessi's energy, the source of the vigour and liveliness that flows along the street like an electric current, are the people of Istanbul themselves, Turks.

And they are neither Eastern nor Western. How, after such a history, could they possibly be just one or the other? Whenever I walked among the tens of thousands of Istanbuliots who streamed along the street such distinctions didn't seem to make any sense at all.

These were people who've become as we've all become – borrowers and adaptors, assimilators and synthesizers of every trend that circles the globe. They were both Eastern and Western at the same time. There were young Kurdish shoeshine boys, smart, skinny street-kids whom I might have labelled 'non-Western'. Then they offered me a shoeshine with a guarantee – three days or ten kilometres, whichever came first. There were pretty, dark Turkish girls who you could have dressed in chadors or headscarves and called Eastern. But they were wearing low-riders and silver jewellery in their belly-buttons. Printed on their T-shirts were Western, in-your-face messages I'd never even seen in the West: '100‰ Hetero'; 'Give Me More'; 'Fabulous Cleavage Under Kit'.

They were part of a constant parade of Turks in whom you could sense a near-infinite genetic mix – it stretched one way through the Balkans and the other way to the Tartar Steppes and a third way through time itself as far as Byzantium. There were a hundred different shapes of eye, tints of hair, curves of cheekbone and nostril. But these were Turks in whom variety went far beyond mere natural selection – they had also made selections from a near-infinite range of big-city lives and lifestyles.

Under sumptuary law in classic Ottoman times each community had worn dress distinguishing it from the other – ethnic Turks wore yellow slippers and red trousers, Greeks black slippers and black trousers, Armenians violet slippers and purple trousers, and so on. Now the ethnic distinctions were gone, replaced by more subtle gradations of cultural difference. Some revolved around bleak questions of survival – even I could spot the newly-arrived migrant job-seeker with his three-day beard and cheap suit. But the Beyoglu side of the Horn tends, as it always has, to sophistication and complexity – there is no part of Istanbul culture as intricate as those sub-genres of youth-culture whose every piece of dress, language and gesture is still part of a code you have to know how to read. Outside certain Beyoglu bars there were people with big Adam's Apples, five o'clock shadow and dresses every bit as gorgeous as the ones worn by the ladies opposite Saint-Benoît. But beyond that particular bit of deciphering I was quickly out of my depth.

No matter. Istanbul had a place for everyone, and I soon made myself comfortable on Istiklal Cadessi and the side-streets that run off it. When Mustafa Kemal proclaimed a republic in 1923 thousands of Beyoglu homes were abandoned by departing Greeks and other minorities. Stuck in legal limbo, some of Istanbul's finest 19th-century architecture was left to rot. There are still blocks of buildings with dark, grimy windows and refuse-covered doorsills, but today their ownership is being renegotiated and all over the quarter smart new art galleries, cafés, bars and clubs are springing up. The after-dark crowds of Beyoglu are even more mixed than the daytime shoppers they replace. It doesn't matter what their

varied origins or lifestyles are. It doesn't matter that
Beyoglu no longer proclaims itself ultra-select. When
drinkers and diners and night-time strollers invade
the quarter they invest it with garrulous sociability –
they bring back much of the Mediterranean passion
and *joie de vivre* it knew a century ago.

And so amidst the outdoor tables that cluttered
street after narrow street, surrounded by fish dinners
and spreads of *mezze* and waiters rushing to replenish
glasses of cold beer, I joined them. With Florent I
discovered obscure bars – kitsch, over-the-top places
frequented by a hip, arty crowd. With Farida I
explored restaurants in Cihangir, a bohemian quarter
of antique shops, elderly ladies feeding stray cats, and
some of Istanbul's last wooden houses. Along with a
couple of hundred admirers of the avant-garde I went
with French friends to watch a local dance performance – it was so experimental I didn't understand a
thing. A few nights later, on the other hand, I was
sitting sipping raki on a sidewalk terrace when not
far away at a dinner-table a woman began to sing. It
was a slow, sad dirge – it was sung in Turkish but was

so poignant, so expressive of the losses and laments known to everyone, that it needed no translation at all. The entire street was held in silent thrall and everyone had goosebumps, including me.

One evening I spent closer to home, in front of a stage set up at the foot of the Galata Tower. A local music group had laid on a free concert. It was as if an Irish rock band had met a Sufi mystic's ensemble head on – the music was an indefinable mix, somehow wholly familiar and utterly strange at the same time. But I had no problem recognising the atmosphere that along with circling seagulls drifted around the spot-lit tower. It was relaxed, sophisticated and tolerant. Spectators lounged on benches, enjoying the cool evening air after the heat of the day. Children played amid sleeping dogs. A young couple, wholly absorbed in each other and oblivious to the world outside, twirled slowly in each other's arms in front of the stage. Was the 800-year-old tower, symbol of a long co-existence, casting around itself some sort of urbane and harmonious influence? The Istanbul that lay below was a cosmopolitan, welcoming place, and I decided I would have no difficulty spending a lifetime there.

But the harmony, I knew, was deceptive. You only had to listen to other voices calling from beyond the tower. Some Turks were knocking hard at the door of Europe; other Turks were urging them to stop and turn back to Islamic ways. East and West, new and old, did not always lie so easily together – all around were other Istanbuls where conflicting strains and tensions were pulling hard in opposite directions. I lay awake a long time in bed that night, watching the seagulls circling the tower through my window and wondering how far its benign influence really extended.

Ten

A day or two later I met a man so pulled by those conflicting strains that they had virtually brought him to a halt. Bekir Cantemir was chief researcher at the *Beyoğlu Arastirmalon Merkezi* – the Beyoglu Municipal Research Centre. It sounded imposing enough, but titles were the most impressive thing about the entire operation. Apart from the polished brass plaque at the door of a building just off Istiklal Cadessi, the place had little to boast of: three narrow floors of mostly bare office space, a few sticks of furniture, a telephone and a handful of staff-members with little to occupy them.

I'd gone there on a wild goose-chase. I was hoping to find an Armenian Turk I'd met at a bus stop on Taksim Square. Waiting together, we'd begun to chat and he had intrigued me immediately. Elderly, a small man with sharp, bright eyes, he was a Catholic priest. He'd been born in Istanbul, grew up in an Armenian monastery in Vienna, and spent a difficult life in voluntary exile abroad – like Jews in Germany a generation later, few Armenians after the great slaughters of 1915 chose to remain in Turkey. Recently, he'd said, he'd finally returned to Istanbul to serve his church as he'd always wanted.

If anyone could tell me about a once-cosmopolitan world attempting to reconstruct itself it was people like this. But before I could ask his name his bus had arrived and he'd been swept off. All I knew was that he officiated in a church in Beyoglu. That didn't make it any easier – if there are few Armenians left in the city there are many Armenian churches. No one I'd spoken to had heard of him. Shrugging his shoulders, one priest had suggested I try the Beyoglu Research Centre.

So now I found myself on a midweek morning in front of three men idly gathered around a desk. Ferruk Arslan, director of the Centre, was a large, powerfully-built man with a broad forehead and a bristly walrus moustache. Even inactive, he radiated physical energy and enthusiasm. Bekir Cantemir was his clever, over-qualified, under-employed right-hand man. Slighter, younger, he was more cerebral than Ferruk – his graduate thesis for the University of the Bosphorus had been an analysis of the Ottoman conception of time. On his dark face there was always a troubled look of polite scepticism, as if he badly wanted to believe but could always find a reason not to. The third man was yet one more Mehmet. He was sharp and quick, but often there was nothing on his face at all – you could feel ennui, an immense, crashing boredom, radiating from him in waves.

No one in the room was about to set an employee-of-the-month performance record. Currently the main interest in the office seemed to be a basil plant sitting in a pot on the desk. Ferruk had bought it at a street cart on the way to work that morning. Turks enjoy greenery and fragrance, and things like basil plants are small treats. Every couple of minutes Mehmet would drape his prayer beads over the rounded top of the plant, taking several runs through the aromatic leaves before languidly sniffing at the beads. Ferruk would occasionally pause in mid-conversation, drop his nose to the plant and take a deep lungful of air. Bekir would run his hands over it, patting delicately as he went, then smooth them over his hair.

'You must smell,' he said when he noticed my curious staring. 'Is it not delicious?' I inhaled and pleased Bekir by agreeing that it was delicious. But I could hardly believe that three grown, educated men were entirely happy to spend their professional careers sitting around sniffing at greenery. There had to be an explanation, and slowly, as I got to know them better over several visits, they gave it to me.

The Research Centre was an office set up and funded by Beyoglu's city hall. 'It is a wonderful project,' said Bekir. 'We are supposed to be collecting the social memory of Beyoglu.' No other place in Turkey, after all, had the same complex, cosmopolitan history. And Ferruk and Bekir had devised many projects to keep that memory alive – everything from archival research facilities to minority language lessons and recitals of traditional Pera music. The Centre had been intended as a hands-on repository of a multi-ethnic Turkey – the basis of Beyoglu's existence under Ottoman rule.

And there lay the problem. I had been in Izmir when elections had brought AK, the conservative Justice and Development party, to power in municipalities throughout Turkey. It had brought them to power in Beyoglu, too. And no matter how far away AK claimed to have moved from its radical Islamist roots, a multi-ethnic Turkey was not part of its vision. AK was more interested in garbage collection than cultural collection, and it had cut back drastically on the research bureau's funding. The whole enterprise was barely limping along. 'Look at our library,' Bekir said gloomily. In the bookshelves above Ferruk's head there were less than a dozen volumes.

But that didn't stop the Beyoglu Municipal Research Centre from searching for a missing person. Ferruk spoke little English and Ahmed none at all, but Bekir conferred with them, explaining my problem. They would be happy to help me, he said; Ferruk knew everyone in Beyoglu, including its Christians.

It might take a day or two to trace the Armenian priest. Would I, in the meanwhile, like to join them for a glass of tea?

And so began a string of mornings in which I would sit around sipping tea, patting the basil plant and discussing the world with Bekir and his colleagues. And for them the world, not surprisingly, had Turkey at its centre – what concerned them most was the way it was changing as the opposing forces of globalisation and Islam bit ever deeper all around them.

We circled each other a little warily at first. Turkish politics are complicated, emotional, sometimes dangerous and never, even in friendly conversation, entered into lightly. Turks take their political engagements personally and passionately.

And no wonder: just eighty ago a radical moderniser had turned an old dynastic world upside down virtually overnight. Suddenly the fez was banned, Arabic script went out the window and Atatürk was foxtrotting around ballroom floors in Western evening wear. Suddenly Turkish women were given the vote years before it came to their French or Italian sisters. All this was dramatic enough. But at the heart of Atatürk's revolution lay two principles that shattered the foundation of Ottoman thought. The first was that all Turkish nationals were only that, Turkish nationals, with no claim to any kind of subsidiary ethnic identity. The second was that religion had no part to play in the public life of a democracy. Few countries have taken a gamble on such rapid and thorough transformation, and the world has watched the Turkish experiment with fascination ever since.

It hasn't always worked smoothly. The Kurds, the country's largest minority, have never been persuaded that they are Turks like any others. And while secular democracy has created a wealthy, Westernised middle-class, the god of Islam will not go away; a much larger numbers of Turks, left far behind and feeling resentful, look to religion for an answer. Sometimes the debate grows hot and heavy – in the last half-century the military, invoking the spirit of Atatürk, have stepped in numerous times to dispense to both radical left and religious right some heavy-handed guidance in the ways of democracy.

Turkish politics flip-flop in all directions, and my new friends had flip-flopped with them. In his socialist youth Ferruk Arslan had been imprisoned, and the other two had been left-wing activists. But now all that was over. To me the greatest irony in the AK's disapproval of the Beyoglu Research Bureau was that all three of these men had now become fervent, practising Muslims. The only time we stopped talking was when they removed their shoes, pushed back the office furniture, and prostrated themselves in the direction of Mecca.

I was taken aback. Ferruk, Bekir and Mehmet had nothing to do with the skull-capped imams I'd heard preaching at Friday prayers in Alexandria. They shared nothing with the peasant-farmers I'd watched emerging from dusty, clay-built mosques in small-town Anatolia. They were modern and educated and they'd undertaken the job of preserving Turkey's cosmopolitan past. But at the same time they were unhappy with the direction the country was heading in.

'Do I surprise you?' Bekir asked me one day. 'Can I not believe in democracy and Islam at the same time? In the West you are free to proclaim your religion if you like, as you are free to proclaim your ethnicity. Can't Turks do the same?

What worried Bekir as much as a disregard for the Turkish past was what he saw as a misappropriation of its future. The more that Turkey became part of the larger world the less control ordinary Turks had over their own lives. For them, he insisted, things were not becoming easier, but harder.

'You've seen the Bosphorus, the beautiful 10 per cent of Istanbul – have you seen how the other 90 per cent of the city lives?' he asked me. 'Every day Ferruk, Mehmet and I sit here debating globalisation, Westernisation, big business, power and profit. Of course Turks want to open up to the world – they have been excluded for a long time. But do you think joining Europe will solve our problems? Europe cannot solve its own problems. Social engineering is not enough. We need social justice.'

I liked Bekir, and at the same time he perplexed

me. He was serious and principled and believed in the need for redress in the world. He had none of the bigot's zealous faith in dogma. But sometimes I thought his idealism hid a deeper fundamentalist streak. One day I asked him if he considered himself an Islamist.

The question made him smile. 'Once I used to dream of a truly egalitarian Turkey.' he said. 'No more. Now I think, Islamist or socialist, it's all the same. The socialists put the people's money into the left-hand pocket. The Islamists put the people's money into the right-hand pocket. It all goes to the same place – to politicians who use power to lead lives of privilege and wealth.' He paused and his tone grew a little wistful. 'What I am,' he said, 'is a Muslim utopian. I am content to believe in ideals that cannot be put into practice. At least not now.'

These were the kinds of discussions we returned to day after day and it wasn't long before I was feeling as befuddled and batted about as the poor basil plant on the table between us.

One afternoon when Bekir and I stepped out of

the office our conversation took a more personal turn. If he could pay more rent, Bekir told me as we sat in a sweet-shop eating plates of halva, nothing could induce him to stay on in Gaziosmanspaşa, the distant western suburb where he and his wife and baby daughter lived.

It was a poor place with few jobs and much frustration. Bekir and his family lived in an apartment, a fifth-floor walk-up that was cramped and hot and noisy. There was no water for most of the day. Bekir wanted to move to a better suburb on the far side of the Bosporus. He would have liked a car so he and his family could escape the city on weekends. And what he really daydreamed about, he confided, was a plot of land in the country where one day he could start an organic fruit and vegetable farm. He shrugged his shoulders – it was just a dream, he said. Muslim utopian or not, Bekir that afternoon seemed to me pretty much like all the rest of us.

The only things he really valued in his apartment were his books. He housed them in custom-built, glass-fronted wooden bookcases. 'You cannot buy bookshelves in Gaziosmanspaşa. I had to have them made,' he told me ruefully. 'Nobody where I live reads. We work if there's work available, we watch television, and we sleep.'

I asked him about the books. He had Islamic histories and sets of religious encyclopaedias printed in Turkish. But for years he'd combed through the flea-markets and second-hand bookstores of Istanbul and also had a surprising number of Western books in English. They included a collection of Marx and volumes by Foucault, Edward Gibbon and Bertrand Russell.

He was especially attached to his works by Marx. 'A great man, a great philosopher,' he said almost fondly as we spooned up sweet semolina patterned with swirls of bright green pistachio. 'In his economic interpretation of history he was the last great spirit in the West to have a complete world-view.'

'Hang on,' I said. 'That's a bit much. Don't you think there have been other thinkers since Marx who ...'

Bekir raised his spoon to stop me.

'It's nothing against the West,' he said conciliatingly. 'We are no more productive of new thought in the East. The last really original Muslim thinker lived 500 years ago. But that's OK. I enjoy him as much as Marx.'

We talked about political extremism and Turkey's frequent recourse to military rule. We talked about Islamists, socialists, communists, nationalists, Kemalists, syndicalists, neo-fascists and Kurdish separatists – all of them active in Istanbul politics. It was hectic and muddled, but Bekir believed that the Turkish obsession with ideology would eventually lead somewhere.

'Positive change will come out of it one day, I am sure, ' he said. 'If the East is merely in the same game as the West, then the only thing that counts anywhere is power and money. But we have other things to offer. If we can contribute our own learning, what will perhaps emerge is a global society, prosperous, but also guided by two things it now lacks – ethics and judgement.'

I had to sit and think about that for a while. I

wasn't a Marxist and I wasn't a Muslim, but Bekir was trying to say something important about the way he saw complex and apparently contradictory ideas coming together to produce new ways of thinking. In the meantime, though, even simple contradictions were enough to slow Bekir to a halt. He was attracted to Western democratic institutions but appalled by the economic excess and greed that came with them. He was enticed by the social justice preached by Islam but repelled by its lack of intellectual freedom. He couldn't give himself entirely to either. In the end, it seemed to me, Bekir was a reflection of something larger – Istanbul itself.

What was an outsider to make of it, this port-city of political ferment and uncertain direction? No one could know the soul of any metropolis after a few weeks' mere strolling around. But at least you could get a working notion of places like Alexandria and Venice. Both were cities of the past. One, ignoring its historical resources, was being swallowed up by it. The other had done something altogether neater – by trading on its past it was holding it at bay.

Istanbul, though, was different. It did not belong to the past alone. It was too vibrant a city, too full of energy and dynamic possibility. It had changed before and it would change again. But it was hard to see which way it was going. There were plenty of signposts indicating the way to Istanbul's future; the problem was that they were pointing in every possible direction. And Bekir was only adding to my confusion. Each time I walked out of the Beyoglu Research Centre I felt more confused about Istanbul than when I walked in.

Eleven

Crash courses in Turkish politics are taxing, and I often felt the need for a quiet place to let things settle. I found it on the Bosphorus just five minutes' walk down the hill from Saint-Benoît.

The Nusretiye, or Victory, Mosque, was clean and peaceful, and even on the warmest afternoon refreshingly cool. I doubt that another tourist had set foot in it for ages. It was a tenth of the size of the Blue Mosque, and squeezed into an old complex of customs buildings not far from the Prince's Islands ferry pier. Outside, endless streams of traffic moved slowly to and from the Galata Bridge on both road and waterways. Inside, seated on the floor beneath a high dome, I had all the calm and open space I needed. The only traffic here came in one concentrated rush, for afternoon prayers, and the muzzein's call to prayer gave me plenty of time to get out of the way.

I liked the mosque for the comfort of lolling about shoeless on a vast expanse of red carpet. But I also liked it because the place sat there like an answer, a concrete resolution of the perplexing contradictions that not just Bekir Cantemir, but the entire city, had thrown up for me.

One had to, granted, overlook the Victory Mosque's original inspiration. Raised long after the great age of Ottoman mosque-building was over, it commemorated a later Sultan's grisly triumph over his own Janissary troops. So resentful were they of the European-style modernisation being imposed on the military, so undisciplined and rebellious had they grown inside the shaky empire, that in 1826 Sultan Mahmud II oversaw the brutal hunting down and extermination of some 5,000 of his elite corps. With their final disbanding, he heaved a sigh of relief and christened the massacre the 'Blessed Event'.

But there was no hint of dissolution about the building itself – it was an extraordinary synthesis.

By that point Western influence in Constantinople had become so pronounced that the mosque's builder had decided on a complete blending of what had become two interdependent traditions. Gone were the austere lines and perfect circles, symbolic of the Islamic infinite, once employed by Sinan, the empire's greatest architect. Instead, like tulip stems growing from their bulbs, minarets grew out of globular, fleshily-rounded stone bases. Pepper-pot towers stood above domes whose lower edges were scalloped into undulating waves. Mullioned windows emerged from curved walls like the poops of Spanish galleons. It was a mosque out of a fevered dream. It was organic, baroque and sensual, a bizarre but happy mix of Islamic asceticism and Counter-Reformation exuberance. It was Santiago de Compostella gone to Mecca.

The builder of the Victory Mosque had been as sophisticated a mix as his creation. Krikor Balian came from a long line of architects serving the Ottoman sultans. From the early 1700s on into the 1900s the Balian family had, generation after generation, changed the face of Constantinople. They built vast palaces, theatres, schools, military barracks, hunting lodges and kiosks – most of the royal architecture, in fact, that can be seen along the Bosphorus today. And they did it in an eclectic, international style. Imperial builders, they were not Turks, but members of one of the most accomplished of Ottoman ethnic minorities, the Armenians.

The Balians intrigued me because they were representative of a cosmopolitan strain present throughout minority groups in the city. From the early 1600s Armenians had arrived in Constantinople in large numbers from eastern Anatolia. They had begun as broom-makers and porters, risen through commercial trade, and a century later attained some of the highest posts in the empire. Architecture aside, they replaced Jews as the city's chief bankers. One Armenian family, the Duzians, were appointed superintendents of the royal mint and kept the post for more than a century. Granted the Ottoman privilege of wearing quilted turbans and riding horses in the city, the Armenian elite oversaw tax collection and government expenditure. They served in the professions, dominated the customs service and became the empire's first modern industrialists – beginning as the Sultan's Chief Gunpowder Makers, the Armenian family of Hovhannes Dadian went on to supply the Ottoman Grand Armies with most of their needs, manufacturing everything from belts and boots to heavy ordnance.

One of Christianity's easternmost peoples, the Armenians were among the empire's most active propagators of Western culture. Ethnic Turks themselves had less interest in trade and the wider contact it brought – they excelled at war, bureaucracy and peasant farming. But the range of minorities promoting exchange between the Ottomans and the rest of the world was as wide as their field of conquest. And like the Armenians, other mercantile minorities not only made up the commercial backbone of empire, but also attained its highest posts.

I'd heard the story, for example, of Constantinople's Jews, a rare and happy one on a continent where violent anti-Semitism was pervasive. Bringing with them expertise in trade, finance, medicine and law when they were evicted from 15th-century Spain, many Jews rose to prominence in imperial service. Chased from Castile in 1492, the Nasis, to name one prominent family, faced continued exclusion as they moved over the next three decades from Portugal to Antwerp and on to Venice, originator of Europe's Jewish ghettos. Joseph Nasi's final move to Constantinople in the mid-1500s changed his fortunes. Developing interests in banking and trade, he became a supplier of both cash and wine to Prince Selim, heir to the throne. On becoming sultan, Selim awarded him the rule of Naxos, a Greek island wrested from Venetian hands and still occupied by a Catholic landowning nobility. Great must have been Joseph Nasi's satisfaction, after a lifetime of humiliation in Christian Europe, to be able at last to call his own tune there.

Or what about Alexander Mavrocordato, an Orthodox Greek born in Constantinople 100 years later? The Greeks were renowned as the craftiest, hardest-driving merchants in the entire empire; Mavrocordato turned out to be one of its finest diplomats.

The first of the city's inhabitants to be sent for an education in Western Europe, he became a physician, a scholar and Grand Logothete in the Greek Patriarchate. His talent with languages soon ensured his promotion to Grand Dragoman. As the Sublime Porte's chief interpreter, he played a vital role in imperial foreign relations. When the Ottomans failed to storm the gates of Vienna at the end of the 1600s it was Mavrocordato who with consummate skill engineered a peace with the Habsburgs – with great tact he made each empire believe that a submissive entreaty for negotiation had been the initiative of the other.

Alexander's son Nicholas, also a Grand Dragoman and fluent in seven languages, went on to assume the throne of Wallachia, an Orthodox Ottoman principality in the Balkans. Like many other prominent ethnic-minority families, the Mavrocordatos had no qualms in serving an imperial master as long as it advanced their personal and community interests. Whether as Greeks, Ottomans or Wallachians, they played whatever card suited them, and sometimes two or more at once. As cosmopolitans, nationality was for them more a professional than a political choice. Possessors of several identities, they would have seen that later historical phenomenon, aggressive and undivided allegiance to a single nation, as limiting and pointless.

All this, of course, took place long before Ottoman institutions had grown rotten to the core, before calls for nationalist insurgence began making violent inroads into the multicultural state. After the Greek revolt the hundreds of thousands of Greeks who remained inside the empire never regarded it in the same way. After the great massacres of civilians in eastern Anatolia during the First World War, Turkish Armenians lost faith in their very survival, much less the possibilities of a larger identity shared with Turks.

In the end nationalist conflicts between the Ottomans and their Greek, Armenian, Serb, Arab and other minorities finished off the empire. Now, as I sat on the carpet beneath a dome that was neither Baroque nor Islamic but both, a question came to mind. What would the Balians or the Mavrocordatos make of today's efforts to build a globalised, multi-national world once again? I couldn't ask them, but the thought occurred to me that I could still ask their cultural descendents. If the Beyoglu Research Centre had as yet failed to trace down one elderly Armenian priest, they had other cosmopolitans on tap.

A day later I was knocking on the door of an upper-floor apartment in the steep streets of Beyoglu below Taksim Square. The man who answered was thin and bald and wore heavy-framed glasses. A spriggy mass of grey beard tumbled over his chest. He held one hand awkwardly in front of himself, and walked with a limp.

'Partial paralysis of the left side – a recent stroke,' he said, leading me into a living room where books, papers and newspaper cuttings cluttered every surface. 'I've had to stop the cigarettes altogether – four packets a day nearly killed me. But I don't want to slow down too much on anything else.'

I could see he meant it. He was a writer bursting with projects, some nearing completion, some well under way, others just taking shape. On a coffee table lay his most recently published book – a thick tome, full of grainy photographs, on the history of Turkish cinema. On the computer screen where he'd been working was the text of one of the three novels he was currently writing.

'And I'm just planning a new collection, short stories of macabre fantasy. I'm calling it *Beyoglu Nightmares*. What do you think?'

What I thought was that Giovanni Scognamillo had more energy and ideas fizzling in his head than most writers half his age. I asked if he thought of himself as a Turkish or Italian writer.

'I write just as easily in either language,' he reflected. 'But as to whether one is more mine than the other...'

He shrugged a shoulder. 'My grandfather was a Neapolitan chef. My mother's family was Greek, but originally came from Genoa. My parents were born here. I was born here. I'm Levantine.

'A lot of people like me don't like the term Levantine. Do you know why? In their minds it's another word for shifty – it's a label attached to someone who cannot be trusted. But I am Levantine, the product of Western Europeans long settled in the East. I don't have a problem with it.'

I, for one, I told Scognamillo, was having plenty of problems. I couldn't get a grip on things in Istanbul. I was confused about the city's cosmoplitan identity, about where it was heading. It seemed to have had one character under the Ottomans, another under Atatürk's republic, and now, as Turkey took up with the wider world, it appeared to be changing again.

'Ah,' said Scognamillo, wagging his beard. 'That's something different, a much larger problem. You're not alone. Every Istanbuliot has the same problem. *I* have the same problem. Some years ago a few fellow-writers and I got together and started a city magazine called *Identity*. But when we got going we realized there's almost nothing in Istanbul that *isn't* a question of identity. So we started to write about everything and anything – impossible, of course – and the magazine soon folded. The city still confuses me.'

I followed the writer into a tiny kitchen where he

prepared coffee so black and strong I started worrying about my own heart. As he rattled cups and saucers I asked him about his interest in Turkish cinema.

'Oh, I've been writing about Turkish films for some while,' he said with a smile. 'I began in 1948 and I'm still at it. My veins are probably made of celluloid by now.'

It had all come naturally, he said. His father had been an importer and distributor of foreign films, and his uncle the owner of a cinema. He virtually grew up in front of a movie screen. He had started as a correspondent for the Italian film press and a decade later, writing for an Istanbul newspaper, become one of the city's most-read film critics.

'Those were busy days in cinema,' he said as I carried a loaded tray out. 'All through the 1960s Turkey was making 180 to 250 films a year. I'm not saying every one was a masterpiece – a lot were B movies. But the industry was thriving, everyone went to the cinema, and it gave Turks a channel for expression they don't have today.'

'Don't Turks watch Turkish films now?'

'Some do. There are some world-quality Turkish directors these days, but only about fifteen Turkish films a year come onto the market. There used to be small independent cinemas in every town and suburb, but they've almost all disappeared. When American studio distributors push 250 copies of the same film into Turkey it is difficult for small movie-makers and small cinemas to survive.'

'Is that what globalisation means for Turkey?'

He sipped coffee and thought about it. 'It means that Turks don't have much choice about becoming more and more like everyone else. It's an inevitable part of the process. When I was younger I used to sell European advertising through the Turkish film distribution system. I stopped it. Why encourage people to buy things they don't need and then work harder and longer to pay for them? They could be enjoying themselves at the movies instead.

'At least at the cinema you are sharing something with the other people there. With computers we are learning to live on our own. Istanbul is still a place where the tradition of close relations with relatives and neighbours is strong. In this building I can ring the bell at any door on any floor – the whole apartment block is one big family I can count on. There is solidarity, communication, participation. Once I was offered a very good job in London, but I soon came back. That kind of exchange has disappeared in other places. It is beginning to disappear here, too.'

We drank coffee. We discussed Beyoglu's once-famous courtesans, the subject of another book the author had written. We watched a torrential summer downpour turn the steep streets outside into raging spates. And when in due course the rain was over and I was at the door shaking his hand, the writer had a last word to say on globalisation. Honest Levantine that he was, Giovanni Scognamillo did not want to leave false impressions.

'I know that many negative changes are on their way to Istanbul,' he said. 'But look.' He lifted his useless arm. 'I can no longer cope with a manual typewriter. So at the same time I am very grateful to my computer. How could I write my friends and colleagues if it weren't for e-mails? How could I compose

Beyoglu Nightmares without a word processor? So I have to admit there are good things that come with change, too. Maybe it doesn't matter if it's the cinema or the computer. Maybe it depends on how these things are used.'

It was hardly a ringing and unqualified endorsement of the global community. Were other Istanbuliots as skeptical as the Italian Turk? The next morning I was at a door in the Syrian Passage, a covered sidestreet off Istiklal Cadessi. Inside, a Greek Turk named Mihaïl Vasiliadis was putting together *Apoyevmatini,* one of the last two last Greek-language newspapers in Istanbul.

Computer technology had not yet come to *Apoyevmatini*. Vasiliadis, his thinning hair slicked away from his forehead, his sleeves rolled up, was leaning forward over a back-lit, plastic-topped counter and laying out his pages with scissors and paste.

'I am a one-man show – I am everything from editor to tea-boy,' he said grinning as I gazed around the two small, bare rooms where he produced the paper every day. 'The only thing I don't have is an editor's or a tea-boy's salary. I don't have any salary at all. Still, the paper keeps going. When I arrived circulation was down to eighty copies a day, the lowest in its eighty-year history. Now we're back up to 500.'

Eighty years, I began to see as we chatted, was nothing in the Vasiliadis time-scale. Even the sack of Constantinople was a relatively recent event in his view.

'To mark the 800th anniversary of the event, the Pope apologised for the greatest disaster ever to hit this city,' said Vasiliadis. 'That's fine. We accept his apology. We do not bear a grudge.'

But Vasiliadis's own family predated the sack by a thousand years. 'My mother's people were not from here. They were Greeks from Macedonia – very tough, very authoritarian. But my father's family!...' He blew out his cheeks and threw up his hand as if even attempting to count the years spent here were useless. 'They were on the Pontic even before the Greeks founded the Pontic Empire. You'd have to go back almost to Adam to find their roots.'

And that was why, he told me as he carefully cut and

fitted small bits of paper together, it was important to remember history. All of it – the disasters, the wars, the bloodshed. If he wanted to preserve the past it was not for the sake of revenge, he said, but to remember its lessons. And remembering sometimes came at a high price.

In 1964 Vasiliadis had been sports editor at the Greek Istanbul newspaper *Eleftherifoni* when it was taken to court for an article it had published on Greek Orthodox minority rights in Turkey. The owner of the paper escaped to Greece. Vasiliadis, who remained, was charged with making propaganda and attacking Turkish national unity.

'The trial lasted ten years,' the editor said wearily. 'Ten years! Two times I was acquitted, and two times the Turkish government brought the same charges against me. Finally, on the third adjudication, I was acquitted for good. I left for Athens and stayed there for twenty-six years.'

'Why bother coming back?'

'Because a century ago our community numbered 200,000. Because today there are only 2,000 ethnic

Greeks left in all of Turkey and only 700 left in Istanbul. If we don't make the effort to keep our language alive and our community connected the numbers will dwindle to nothing. Without things like this paper we will disappear.'

Was the task easier or more difficult, I asked, than it was back in the 1960s?

'Oh, it's much better now. Turkey is getting closer to Europe all the time. That is not because the Europeans accept and welcome Turkish culture, but because the Turks accept to become more like Europeans. And one thing Europe demands is the protection of minority rights. When Turkey learns to accept its own minorities, then it, too, will be accepted as a minority.'

So overall, I suggested, globalisation was moving things in a positive direction.

'Perhaps not,' Vasiliadis replied, removing his mock-up from the counter and inspecting it beneath the room's fluorescent lighting. 'It's becoming harder to hold any small community together these days. We Greeks have bad teachers right in our living rooms – our televisions. They tell our people to do the opposite of what our traditions tells us. Action movies, MTV, narcotics, sex, one generation set against another – none of these are going to help the last Greek Orthodox families of Istanbul.'

And was there nothing, I asked, to fight back with?

'Of course. There is a very old, very powerful weapon against all cultural transformation,' the editor said. 'It is the manipulation of race and religion by violent extremists. And we have all seen what it can do. When you are faced with two evils you choose the lesser. So we watch Pamela Anderson Lee.'

Here, then, was one more doubter, another man not entirely convinced of the benefits of an ever smaller and more connected world. Mihaïl Vasiliadis left the office to take the day's edition of *Apoyevmatini* to the printer's, and I strolled back to Bekir Cantemir wondering if Istanbul really had any cosmopolitan future at all.

'Good news!' said Bekir over a now mangled and fast-wilting basil plant. 'Ferruk has found your priest.

His name is Father Aygaram and he can be found at the Saint John Crysostome Armenian Church. He holds a communion service there every day and a full mass on Sundays. I hope he can tell you what you want to know.'

There was deep silence when I slipped in through the doors of the church the next morning. Not far from the Palais de France in old Pera, it was an elegant building, the dome over its apse decorated in glowing blue and gold. There were columns with imitation marble veining, a crowned Christ over the altar, and a crystal chandelier hanging from a great height. It wasn't lit, but instead caught the rays of morning sun that penetrated the church's tinted windows. Every piece of glass scintillated. The only thing missing was a congregation. There wasn't a single church-goer in Saint John Crysostome to take part in Father Aygaram's service.

But there was the man I had met on Taksim Square, the small priest with the sharp, bright eyes. Alone in the midst of all this splendour, he looked smaller still. He stood at a side-chapel beneath an oil-painted Pieta whose Virgin Mary bore a raised heart of embossed silver. He paid no attention to the empty church behind him, but, back turned to the pews, proceeded with a communion at which he was the only celebrant. Dressed in a white robe with a high collar and a gold cross embroidered on its back, he read in a firm, strong voice from an Armenian text sitting on an altar. He polished chalices, poured wine, broke and offered himself the host with all the decorum of a man officiating before a great crowd.

I thought he was magnificent, more impressive in his own way than Krikor Balian himself. Here was a man who'd been isolated from his community all his life. He had returned to serve a church so decimated by a bloody, genocidal past that not a single worshipper had turned up for a weekday service. And yet he carried on regardless, so persistent in his own conviction, sure enough in the spirit if not the substance of his people, that he considered the whole effort worthwhile. If this man could start trying to rebuild a once flourishing, multicultural world in which community identity was the touchstone, then anyone could.

Without asking anything, I stole quietly out of the church before the service was over. Father Aygaram had answered my questions without having to say a word.

Twelve

Barrel-chested Ferruk Arslan, I discovered, had two passions. One was the history of Beyoglu. The other was fishing.

I discovered this on a Monday morning when I was telling Bekir about the fishermen I'd seen on the Galata Bridge the day before. On weekends it isn't just the bars and restaurants on the bridge's lower level that fill to capacity. The sidewalks on each side of the tarmac above them get crowded, too. From early morning until after sunset the bridge bristles with fishing rods. Istanbuliots are among the most enthusiastic big-city catchers of small fish in the world. It isn't just the urban poor seeking inexpensive leisure who indulge – all sorts of people stand elbow to elbow at the bridge railing each weekend. Nor are

ISTANBUL 07

they put off by the modest size of the catches on offer at the mouth of the Golden Horn. The little creatures they collect in bowls and plastic tubs to take home alive are scad, a saltwater fish also known as horse mackerel. Sea-going tiddlers, they measure between four and six inches each.

Nobody cares. When scad are running up the Bosphorus from the Mediterranean to the Black Sea you can haul up half a dozen on a multi-hooked line at one time. Watching little fish rise wriggling and flashing, one after another, only to mysteriously disappear into the heavens above is one of the privileges of the beer-drinkers lounging on the level below. There had been so many fishermen on Sunday afternoon that as I crossed the bridge I'd made a count – there were 327 of them on my side of the bridge alone, and at least as many on the other.

'Just imagine,' I was saying to Bekir as we sat over glasses of tea with Ferruk and Mehmet the next morning, 'that's about 650 people on the bridge fishing for scad.'

Ferruk, who usually sat through our conversations

impassive and understanding nothing until Bekir made a translation, suddenly sat up.

'Scad,' he said, beaming. 'English, scad. Turkish, "*istavrit*." Latin, "*trachurus trachurus*."'

Ferruk seemed to be a linguistic master when it came to fishing.

'How about mullet?' I said, testing him.

'English, red mullet. Turkish, "*barbunya*". Latin, "*mullus barbatus*."'

This was astonishing. 'What about "lure"?' ' I said, switching to fishing tackle in a effort to throw him. 'Do you know what a lure is?'

'Lure!' he crowed. 'Red Devil, Mister Twister, Shad Rap, Silver Minnow, William's Wobbler, Rappala Husky Jerk, Blue Fox Super Vibrax Spinner, Bionic Bait Jig Combo...'

'Ferruk!' I said, interrupting a non-stop flow, 'You're an expert!' His face broke into a wide grin. If I hadn't stopped him he might have gone on forever.

It turned out he really was an expert – there was little Ferruk didn't know about Mediterranean fishing. If he knew English fishing terms it was because he corresponded with various scientific fishing research institutes and had a fishing library much larger than the Beyoglu Research Centre's cultural library. But his interest weren't just academic. Ferruk had actually built ancient Mediterranean fishing craft. He had experimented with antique methods of fish-netting and trapping known in classical times. And he loved to eat fish and seafood – Ferruk caught and consumed everything that finned, wriggled or crawled its way about the water.

Was there something hidden deep in his genetic memory? Ferruk wasn't descended from the horse-riding plainsmen of the Asian steppe. His ancestors were true Mediterraneans, shore dwellers from the coast of Albania. Whatever it was, his enthusiasm was infectious. Through Bekir we talked fish for half the morning, and by 11 o'clock he had set me up with a fishing trip.

He had wanted to send me to join the fishing fleet down on the Turkish Mediterranean coast, for it was now swordfishing season there. 'Big fish,' he said, holding his arm in front of his nose and making a spear of it. But that would mean an outing lasting at least a couple of weeks, and it was more time than I had. In the end Ferruk telephoned Ismail and Mumtaz, both friends of his and assistant managers at Istanbul's wholesale fish market. I was going fishing on the Sea of Marmara.

Early next afternoon I walked back over the Galata Bridge, across Seraglio Point and along the Marmara shore towards Kumkapi. There were fish everywhere – fish piled on ice in the display cases of waterfront restaurants, fish flipping in baskets beside wrinkled old men casting from the rocks. They were even fish lying fifty yards offshore in the bottom of a styrofoam shell, once protective packing for a refrigerator, today an improvised fishing boat used by two small and intrepid boys jigging with handlines.

I met Ismail and Mumtaz in an echoing hall, white-tiled and brightly-lit, where much of Istanbul's commercial catch is sold to fishmongers and restaurant owners. Workmen were hosing down floors and walls and the two assistant managers were removing the white coats that made them look like lab researchers.

They were just as professional-looking in the crisp white shirts and ties that lay underneath.

I thought Ismail and Mumtaz were going to pass me on to some regular fishermen, for they were now at the end of a long workday – in Istanbul the boats arrive at two o'clock in the morning and the market opens at four. But instead they changed into old work clothes and we drove a couple of miles down the shore to a small boat-harbour. There we hopped into the *Oguz,* a 26-foot wooden vessel with a small forward cabin and a thumping diesel engine.

'Before we fished,' said Ismail.

'Now we work in an office with pens and tele-phones,' added Mumtaz.

'Wives and children at the weekends,' intoned Ismail.

'We miss the boats and the sea,' lamented Mumtaz.

Both looked far happier in old clothing covered in engine oil and dried fish scales than they had in their lab-coats. There was a strong breeze blowing down the Bosphorus and it whipped up their neatly combed hair and the little star-and-crescent Turkish flag blowing from the boat's bow. Mumtaz gripped the wheel and Ismail and I wedged ourselves into corners in the stern – as soon as we left the harbour the *Oguz* began ploughing into white-capped waves.

'This wind is from the north – it is called the Poyras,' Mumtaz turned back to me. With the wind singing and the engine banging away below he had to shout. 'It is the best wind for Istanbul fishermen. After blowing out of the Bosphorus it has no time or space to become rough. The other wind, the Lodos, is from the south. It is dangerous – long swells, big waves. It can sink fishing boats even in port and blow big ships onto the shore.'

I didn't mind the fresh and lively Poyras even if it was bucketing our little boat up and down. It was good to get away from the unending crowds and the heat of the street. It was good to get away, too, from all the difficult questions hanging over the city. From here Istanbul looked like what it had always been, one of the great seaports of the world. Each year 50,000 ships steered a course straight through the middle of the metropolis; slowly we were now making our way among a couple of dozen of them, moored tankers and freighters with their anchor-chains hauled tight and their bows pointed into the wind. Behind them I could see Istanbul, its minarets rising above the city, and beyond, higher still on the far side of the Bosphorus, the green hills of Anatolia.

Half an hour later we had drawn even with Yedikule, the stone-towered fortress that sits where the city's old Byzantine land-walls meet the sea. A mile offshore, Mumtaz set the *Oguz* turning in wide circles and Ismail went into the little cabin to get the equipment. What were we going to fish for, I wondered? It wasn't going to be swordfish, but in Istanbul markets I had admired other large and handsome creatures. Was it going to be bluefish? Bonito?

Ismail came back on deck with a couple of blocks of wood around which were wound thin nylon line carrying dozens of miniscule feathered hooks. Bonito would just laugh at this kind of gear. I had the sinking feeling that I had seen this kind of equipment before.

'*Istavrit*!' smiled Ismail. 'We will catch many, many fish!'

I smiled bravely back. We might as well be jigging from floating refrigerator-packing. It was not going to be a trophy-fishing day.

But Ismail was right. There were scads of scad. We seemed to be in the middle of thick schools running intermittently for the Bosphorus. First there would be nothing, then we would be hauling line madly for a few minutes, pulling in eight or ten fish at a time. Then all would go all quiet, giving us a chance to collect the little creatures flopping about the floor of the boat. The wind blew, the boat circled beneath a bright sun, the fish came in fits and starts and I forgot our prey were scarcely larger than minnows. I was having fun. Before I knew it the afternoon had melted away and we were headed back to the harbour. At the stern of the boat lay a basket filled with hundreds of little silver fish.

What were we going to do with them? To me they looked too small and bony to make eating anything but a problem. But I had not reckoned on the talents of Mumtaz and Ismail.

A few yards from where we docked the *Oguz* we set up chairs around an empty drum of heavy-duty electrical cable laid on its side. This was a working-man's harbour and the waterside looked like a marine junkyard. Around us were men fiddling over the open bonnets of their cars, men messing with outboard motors, men tinkering with fish-finders and other electrical equipment. Greasy bits of machinery and old engine parts lay scattered everywhere. There were dented barrels of marine fuel stacked on an oil-stained quay and socks and wet-weather gear strung on lines to dry. I might even have seen a rat or two climbing about some coils of old rope. As dining décor went it hardly matched the elegant fish restaurants that sat beside the water around Istanbul.

We spent half an hour gutting. It's not difficult snapping scad-heads off between your thumb and forefinger and gently pulling out their innards. After you've done four or five dozen it doesn't seem such a bad job at all. Still, I didn't think these little animals were going to make much of a meal. But from his storage shed Ismail dug out a small gas canister and ring, a frying pan and some cooking oil, and set to. Having heated and salted a good amount of oil, he quickly rolled a batch of twenty or so fish in a plate of flour before dropping them into the pan where they sat sizzling and turning gold. In the meantime Mumtaz set out a tablecloth from the pages of *Milliyet*, the Turkish daily, on the cable-drum table. From the boot of his car he returned with loaves of fresh bread, and into a tin plate he cut tomatoes, onions and dark purple shallots. There was also a cooler containing bottles of ice-cold Efes beer, and once he'd snapped off the caps of three of them we were in business.

I couldn't remember a fish dinner I'd enjoyed as much. Almost too hot to hold, we squeezed lemon juice onto the little fish, dipped them in salt, and popped them in our mouths. They were crisp outside and tender inside, and full of delicate flavour. Now I knew why so many fishermen stood on the Galata Bridge each weekend and carefully guarded their little prizes until they could carry them home still swimming. There is nothing quite as good as fresh scad you've caught and cooked yourself.

A bite of fish, a little salad, a sip of beer, a hunk of bread torn from a loaf ... as soon as we'd polished off one batch of scad the next was being fished from the spitting pan. Not only was the meal memorable – it wasn't long, in fact, before I decided that I couldn't think of surroundings more congenial to consume it in.

The cluttered concrete quay, the sheds and drying clothes, the boats flying their red Turkish flags ... all these ordinary things took on animation and life as other small-boat fishermen returned from a day on the water and began filling the port. There was still plenty of fish to eat, and soon our round table was surrounded by a half a dozen bristly-chinned fishermen. They were rough and raw and full of broad banter, but more than friendly to the foreigner who couldn't speak three words of their language. They slapped my back and encouraged me to take more food and drink. Here, of course, was the real attraction of these surroundings – generous, ordinary working people happy to share their lives with an unknown stranger.

Could they be called cosmopolitans? Hardly.

Did it matter how Ismail and Mumtaz and their fishing friends fit into the complex puzzle of Istanbul politics? Not really. As I finished off my last little scad the labels seemed unimportant. What counted was the exchange.

On the point of leaving, I received an invitation from a friend of Ismail's, a brawny, ham-handed man named Namuk. He was leaving the next afternoon on a four-day fishing trip to the distant middle reaches of the Sea of Marmara. I was welcome to go with him. '*Büyük balik!*' he said, using one of those calloused hands to measure on his other arm an imaginary fish running from fingertips to biceps. Big fish. Brave on beer and bonhomie, I was all ready to accept Namuk's offer when Ismail took me to one side.

'How did you like the sea on the *Oguz* today?' he asked.

'It was fine,' I said, remembering the boat pounding hard enough into each wave to make the hull shiver.

'Good,' said Ismail. 'Because Namuk's boat is even smaller than the *Oguz*. But the waves out in the middle of the Marmara Sea are bigger – much bigger. You will be three nights out there. And a Poyras does hot hold forever – the wind can shift and become a Lodos. Then the sea is something else. Then I am happy I am not a fisherman with nets and a boat, but an assistant manager with pens and a telephone. Think of a little boat in big wind before you decide.'

So I did, and it sobered me up. It also made me think that Istanbul must be a strange and powerful place. It affected everything, even the wind that blew over it. The weather here was like the city itself. It was changeable and difficult to predict. It had two dispositions. It could veer between extremes. If I was going to sit and quietly contemplate the city one last time, it was probably better not done from the heaving deck of a small boat in a fierce blow. There was another place on the water I knew of, and not even the fiercest gale could capsize it. It was a bridge.

Thirteen

Like maritime trading routes, those invisible bridges that have spanned the liquid continent for centuries, the Galata Bridge spans the Golden Horn and holds the city fast. And like those routes it, too, carries a wealth of freight, much of which is not material at all, but symbolic of the greater life of the city.

By 1845, the year the first Galata pontoon-bridge was opened, its pedestrians were already long accustomed to their cosmopolitan existence. Among the crowds that bustled daily along its floating, bobbing length, an endless variety of peoples could be seen. They were resplendent in every gradation of colour, from the white kilts and velvet waistcoats of the Albanians to the black tunics and tall sheepskin headdresses of the Circassians. There were still Ottoman officials from distant places, provincial dignitaries visiting the capital to inspect its wonders, who strolled over the new bridge swathed in turbans and flowing, floral-patterned robes. But already official Istanbul had abandoned traditional wear – the carriage-borne emissaries who clattered over the water from the Sublime Porte to the embassies of Pera now wore the stambouline, the dark, form-fitting frock-coat that made them look more like English country parsons than Ottoman functionaries.

More than a century and a half later, the Galata Bridge is still the focal point of the city and a barometer of both its constancy and its change. Enlarged in the 1860s, rebuilt with a row of shops and restaurants slung beneath it in the following decade, rebuilt yet again after the turn of the new century, the bridge remained a floating bridge, supported on steel pontoons, long after such constructions had disappeared from other ports around the world. And if the much-used eating and drinking places on its lower level became more ramshackle and less elegant as each decade went by, they were cherished by Istanbul's fond citizens as institutions that had become part of the very essence of their city. No evening was as cosmopolitan as a conversation-laden evening spent at a well-garnished table suspended over the waters of the Golden Horn.

In the early 1990s the old bridge was finally done away with. Its pontoons interfered with the flow of Bosphorus waters in and out of the Horn, and steadily rising levels of pollution threatened to turn the inlet into a sewer. The new Galata Bridge, a larger structure raised on fixed pilings, was perhaps more efficient in allowing the free passage of water. But not only did the blocky span of battleship-grey steel fail to charm Istanbuliots; it threatened the free flow of other liquids. No sooner were the new fish restaurants and bars built on its underside opened than the city's first Islamic municipality pledged to have the serving of alcohol in the city's public places prohibited. It would have meant the end of life as it had long been known and loved on the Galata Bridge.

But Istanbul's long tradition of tolerance continued

to hold sway. In the end the alcohol ban, along with a series of other anticipated Islamising measures, failed to materialise. The new mayor ended up infuriating his hard-line supporters. Instead of bringing on the minor Islamic earthquake he had promised he did his best to present Istanbul as a modern, broad-minded, international city. It was one more example of old, moderating Mediterranean influences still subtly at work. Finally it wasn't the Islamists who were conquering Istanbul, exalted the city's more liberal inhabitants, but Istanbul which was conquering the Islamists.

So it was that on my last afternoon in Istanbul I could stroll down the hill from Saint-Benoît and in the middle of the Galata Bridge order a tall, cold glass of beer. I had my air-ticket to Marseilles and home. My bags were packed. I had made my goodbyes to Bekir and Ferruk and Mehmet, to Farida and Florent and their friends. I had a taxi booked to drive me to the airport for a 5.00 a.m. flight the next morning. And now I had the leisure to watch the afternoon sun sink into the Horn and the night to steal one last time over the city.

On late summer afternoons most people like to sit on the terraces on the shady, eastern side of the bridge, the side open to the Bosphorus. It's cooler, and there is the constant spectacle of big boats ploughing their way up and down between the Mediterranean and the Black Sea. But on this afternoon I chose a waterside table and the spectacle of little boats on the western, sunset side of the bridge. I wanted to see what I had seen on my first afternoon here.

And I wasn't disappointed. As I sipped beer and watched little fishes rise wriggling and flashing on the lines of the fishermen above me, the wind slowly died and the air became still. Growing larger as it dropped, a tangerine-coloured sun dipped to the horizon and the water and the world surrounding it were caught in glittering, rippling light. The Horn was golden once again. The small boats crawling their way from one side to another; the rounded domes of the mosques; the little figures strolling on the Horn's banks – all glowed bright and luminous, as if lit from inside. Everything was in stasis, each object centred around its own pulsing, interior life. A calm, or a least the only kind of calm a place like Istanbul can know, descended on the city. For a brief instant it looked like nothing in the city had ever changed or ever would.

It was all illusion, of course, a play of light upon water. Istanbul was always changing. I had finally decided that it was all right to feel perplexed by the city. So frequent and widespread were its mutations, so great its contradictions, that the city felt constantly perplexed about itself. Istanbul had been too many different things, was too many different things now, for it to have a single, fixed identity. Anyone who arrived at a set definition of the place was missing its point. Continuous exchange, transformation and diversity are its point. In that it was no different from many other cities around the liquid continent.

But Istanbul had been something else as well. It had been the very heart of the cosmopolitanism that had once made up the eastern Mediterranean. From here a type of globalisation profoundly different from our own, the Ottoman *millet*, had radiated out to make up one of the world's most sophisticated and accomplished societies. It was all very long ago.

Did it mean anything at all now, I wondered? Did a system of multinational management that guaranteed identity in return for cohesion hold anything for us today?

I thought of New York and London and Paris, of sidewalks and subways packed with people of every race on earth. In so far as most of us in the Western world have largely given up religious and ethnic identification and no longer bow to autocrats, such a system has nothing to offer us directly. These days we define ourselves by our economic standing and the cultural life we share with our peers, regardless of origins. And that, we say, is one of the great benefits of globalisation – at last we are getting over the crude differences of race and religion. And in terms of the worst excesses of nationalism, perhaps we are. But as I sat there watching the glow over the Golden Horn slowly subside I could think of a few things the old Ottoman cosmopolitans might be whispering to us if we chose to hear them.

Over the last half-century, they'd be saying, we have at last seized a Red Apple of our own – in our modern way we have conquered the world. We've evolved global financial institutions that make the wealth-creation of the Grand Viziers look paltry. We've devised global communications that are faster than any crack unit of Janissaries on the march. And we have developed a world-wide network of trade and commerce that even the most ambitious merchants of Istanbul would have never believed possible. All have permitted huge advances in a process of human inter-connection that the Ottomans themselves long ago dreamed of in other forms and for other purposes.

But if we are coming close to creating a truly global economy, the old Istanbuliots would say, we've messed up badly in creating a global identity to go with it. There our thinking is not world-wide at all, but reverts to the same state of mind, compartmental and ethnocentric, that has formed our outlook for the last 300 years.

In the developed West we have reached a point of economic well-being where appeals to the security provided by shared race and religion no longer promise much benefit. It is harder for us to see the reassurance that such promises still provide in other, not-so-prosperous, non-Western societies. Not only does the rationale of the global marketplace allow us to reshape traditional economies without batting an eyelid. Without even noticing it we allow those same forces to run rough-shod over traditional identities – not over an economy-based identity like our own, but over religious and ethnic identities. And when those religions and ethnicities turn in on themselves in an attempt at self-preservation we say we don't understand why they hate us.

'Just think of it!' I could imagine a party of cushion-bolstered *kapi kulu* saying as their *caique*, lit by flickering lanterns and propelled by fez-topped rowers, slid through the waters of the Horn in the growing dusk. 'It would be like the Turks expecting all the empire's different communities to abandon everything and behave like just them. Can you imagine an Orthodox Christian Montenegrin fasting at Ramadan?' Can you see a wild Nubian from the upper Nile wearing flowered muslin? A Crimean Tartar speaking Ottoman Turk? A Bedouin nomad giving up his flocks? An Albanian mountain brigand abandoning his code of honour? No self-respecting Ottoman would dream of asking such things. Small wonder there's rebellion in the ranks.'

But suppose for a moment, just suppose, a cosmopolitan Krikor Balian or Alexander Mavrocordato might say, that something like the *millet* was operating in the globalisation process today. What if different communities in a fast-changing and unpredictable world were encouraged to hang on to what they feared for most, their identities? What if the recognition of those identities, accompanied by genuine participation in the larger world community, permitted the sharing of a larger, compound identity as well? And what if the economic and other rewards of that participation were sufficient that every group was prepared to answer to an authority superior to them all?

I realized, as I sat there daydreaming and watching night slowly fall on the city, what I was imagining: an authentically cosmopolitan world, a system based on a single global commerce and multiple global identities. Was the idea of world government – for that, in effect, is what it would amount to – too starry-eyed and innocent of the realities of international capital and power to be plausible? In our own particular vision of globalisation, fuelled by the hardnosed *realpolitik* of commercial competition alone, nothing has been easier than the violent manipulation of racial and religious fears. Has *that* been practical? It is not just exotic and distant populations who can answer that question. One could also ask the people of New York, London and Paris, those who have known the blind destructiveness of modern terrorism.

It is not only disintegrating societies that need a stake in a changing world. Today all of us are uprooted, all of us are potential cosmopolitans. The Ottomans would have seen plurality as a natural answer in the present world, insisting that if one identity weren't enough, well then, two or three might resolve the problem. But as I sat there listening to night whispers, my ear cocked for what the old city's sophisticates might have said, there were other, cautionary voices as well.

'We just weren't careful enough. We let ourselves

become greedy,' I seemed to hear, although it could have just been the tipplers behind me pondering, too late, the wisdom of drinking double rakis. 'Obviously there is a certain style to live up to in a world capital like Constantinople. *Caiques* and *yali*s and pleasure-kiosks cost money. But we became self-serving. We sucked up the empire's wealth. We paid no attention to poor and distant rural areas. We stepped too hard on the peasantry. We ignored local needs. We forgot civic institutions. Naturally people got fed up. In the end the Ottomans got what they deserved.'

'We weren't as bad as the Alexandrians,' I heard a dissenting voice cut in. 'They bought all the cotton they could get their hands on and got rich selling it to the rest of the world. Did they ever think about cutting the Egyptians in? No wonder that fellow Nasser looked so good. Everyone gets their share, or things fall apart. And speaking of sharing, pass back that hookah, would you?'

Were the voices rising into the cool night air coming from somewhere beneath the underside of the bridge? Maybe it was just a few fishermen, happy to

236

be rowing home at the end of a long afternoon's scad-fishing. Now another voice rose out of the darkness.

'If only we could start all over again,' it said wistfully. 'We didn't know it, but of course we were doomed from the beginning. Continual war and conquest – that's what the whole thing depended on. These other globalists, the ones chasing after markets, buying and selling every resource they can lay their hands on – they think they can carry on indefinitely. It can't be done – we reached our limit and at some point they'll reach theirs. You can only take something out if you put something back in. I believe these days they call it "sustainability".'

'Gentlemen!' there was a sudden loud harrumph-ing, although once again I couldn't be sure – perhaps it was only a ferry horn announcing an evening departure to Üsküdar. 'Gentlemen! All this talk of putting in and taking out is a waste of time. We're old men. We couldn't keep anything sustained for a single minute. But at least we have our old men's fancies. The night is young – what do you say we ride around Seraglio Point and float down to my cousin

Yusef's *yali* at Yedikule? He tells me he's got the most delightful new dancing-girls, one from Tabriz, the other Crimean. It might be amusing. What do you say?'

There seemed to be a clamour of general accord, a splashing of oars, and with that the voices faded away. The only noise now was the noise of the modern Istanbul night.

Does any generation listen to any earlier generation, whatever the issue? Perhaps we are so certain that the world we're rushing into is so new and so different that the past cannot possibly hold anything for us. I didn't believe it. More than ever I had the certainty it was the same old world. But I was under no illusion that ancient Ottoman voices would ever have the ears of today's movers and shakers – even if the entire A-list at Davos were to come and sit themselves down on the Galata Bridge and listen hard I doubt they'd hear anything at all.

I reached the end of the bridge and began climbing the steep hill to Saint-Benoît. In some ways it didn't matter if Davos listened or not. A cosmopolitan attitude to the world cannot simply be dictated. But then neither can its opposite. I thought of Mimi Awad and the winged god Nike perched on the statue of Alexander; of Lotfi the Tunisian racing sleepless night and day for Damascus; of a Syrian sea-captain ranting wildly into the Latakia night; of bear-like Gianfranco Vianelli rising to the defense of the Venetian gondola; of a French mathematics teacher travelling to the far end of the sea to recover her identity; of a small, sharp-eyed priest disregarding the emptiness of a large church to assert his own identity. The Mediterraneans I'd met in the last six months had too much vitality to let their world become the place we fear it might. For them it was still rich in variety and human possibility. Didn't the culture of the old Mediterranean we so much admire today grow out of times as unpredictable as our own?

And the greatest unpredictability lay right in this city, at the place where one day many worlds might meet and, again, fuse. Where is that place? I am sure it isn't, as the guidebooks insist, merely the spot where two continents come together on the shores of

Bosphorus. What did Bekir Cantemir mean when he talked about a global existence guided by two things it now lacks – ethics and judgement? Perhaps that is the place. I thought about it walking slowly up the steep hill, and I think about it still.

Reference Notes

Part of the vast literature of the history of the eastern Mediterranean, I have quoted from the following handful of books, indispensable to any sensible view of three global cities.

1) A historian of court-life and dynasties, Philip Mansel excels in describing the cosmopolitan nature of Ottoman rule in *Istanbul – City of the World's Desire, 1453–1924* (Penguin: 1997). The Duke of Wellington's pronouncements on the empire's usefulness to European powers, which I have quoted, appear in Mansel's pages; so do Lady Mary Wortley Montagu's comments on the ethnic mix of her many grooms and footservants. I have also borrowed from Mansel's depiction of Galata social life and entertainment in

both early and later Ottoman times; from his descriptions of mid-19th century sartorial fashions to be seen on the Galata Bridge, and from his accounts of Armenian, Greek and Jewish ethnic-minority families in the public life of Constantinople.

2) I also owe a debt to Jason Goodwin, author of *Lords of the Horizons – A History of the Ottoman Empire* (Vintage: 1999); in poetic, kaleidoscopic fashion he captures not only the history but the minds of the Ottomans. Especially helpful were his accounts of the myth of the Red Apple; of the Ottoman conception of war; of the ingenuity of the Kapi Kulu system; and of the reasons for the military and administrative decline of the empire.